WHAT I MEAN WHEN I SAY I'M AUTISTIC

"Annie Kotowicz has given us a great gift with this book—to describe, validate, translate, and celebrate the beauty and complexity of an autistic experience.

"The way she describes it is so beautifully clear, elegant, and precise. It models a creative, positive self-understanding that is inspirational regardless of one's neurotype.

"This is not just a model for autistic folks learning to love themselves and to self-advocate, but also helps all of us see the beauty, the importance, and the art of learning about oneself—it helps us understand other people better, too. Every page is a gem."

— **Cathy Robertson**
Founder & Director of *DC Peers*

"I highly recommend Annie's book. It is very readable and relatable. The book will allow others to both relate to and understand the autistic experience in a better way through Annie's explanation of both theory and her own experiences."

— **Sarah Hendrickx**
Author of *Women and Girls with Autism Spectrum Disorder*

"A remarkable journey to a deeper understanding of what autism can feel like from the inside. Annie Kotowicz's curiosity, wonder, and wisdom—beautifully conveyed through her exquisite prose— provide insight and guidance that will help you connect more deeply with the neurodivergent people in your life."

— **Sarah Wayland, Ph.D.**
Co-author of *Is This Autism? A Guide for Clinicians*,
Founder of *Guiding Exceptional Parents*, and
Co-founder of *The Behavior Revolution*

First Edition

ISBN: 979-8-9864827-1-2 (paperback)
ISBN: 979-8-9864827-2-9 (hardcover)
ISBN: 979-8-9864827-0-5 (ebook)

Library of Congress Control Number: 2022911768

Published by Neurobeautiful™
neurobeautiful.com
Rockville, MD

WHAT I MEAN WHEN I SAY I'M AUTISTIC

Unpuzzling a Life on the
Autism Spectrum

ANNIE KOTOWICZ

Neurobeautiful

Contents

Introduction

Why This Matters

There are thousands of us—women who discovered our autism well into adulthood, well past many of the memories it explains. We're too late in life to prevent a multitude of misunderstandings, yet too early in history to say, "I am autistic!" and trust that everyone will know what we mean. We need to unpuzzle the past to heal our hearts, and the present to see who we are.

There are millions of us—autistic people of all ages and genders, trying to make ourselves understood, trying to survive as sensitive souls in an unwelcoming world. We're hardly ever fully at ease, and hardly ever fully ourselves. We need to unpuzzle our behavior so that people will recognize our reasons, and our rights.

There are billions of us—humans everywhere, with access to our own minds and no one else's, tossing one another songs and sentences to bridge the gap. We're endlessly experimenting with new ways to translate our experiences, and listening curiously as others experiment, too. We need to unpuzzle one another, and it becomes easier the more we unpuzzle ourselves.

Yet there is only one me, and this is my story. Not the whole story of a life, but parts of it—the parts that best illuminate what I mean when I say I'm autistic, and the parts that were most puzzling before I discovered this crucial fact about myself.

1

Maybe you'll see yourself reflected in these pages. Maybe you won't, even if you are autistic. Maybe you'll see a palette of possibilities for what people you love might be feeling, or maybe you'll doubt that I could possibly have a mind like theirs.

Maybe you'll underline what resonates, and cross out what doesn't, before handing the book to someone else to understand you better. Maybe, like me, you've been wounded by the stereotype of autism as a puzzle, or at least the implication that we're impossible to understand.

I've spent five years trying to undo that assumption, writing posts and articles under the pen name "Neurobeautiful." For two of those years, I also worked at a school where most of the students are autistic. There, I tried to figure out which of my experiences are caused by autism, and which are merely me.

I eventually concluded that there's no difference between the two. Autism affects all of my experiences, but it does so in ways that are unique to me. Others may be similar—more similar than we appear from the outside—but no two minds are identical, even if we share the same neurotype.

In spite of the wide variety across the autism spectrum, I hope that this book will give you a way to interpret any autistic behavior through the lens of neuroscience. I've applied my understanding of autism to personal stories, but this is more than a memoir. It's also a model of how autism works, a mirror of how autism can feel, and a manifesto celebrating the beauty of autistic brains.

Prologue

A Conversation with Little Me

Me: "You look kind of grumpy."

Little Me: "Yeah, a teacher was mean to me."

Me: "What happened?"

Little Me: "I was using my hula hoop as a jump rope, and he yelled, STOP THAT!"

Me: "Wait... as a jump rope?"

Little Me: "I mean, holding it in front of me, and stepping through, and then flipping it back over my head so I can step through again."

Me: "Sounds fun."

Little Me: "I do it all the time at recess, but he wouldn't let me do it in the hallway."

Me: "Ah, see, that makes sense. Because you could hit someone."

Little Me: "But he acted like I broke a rule! Nobody told me it was a rule."

Me: "There are a bunch of rules that no one will ever tell you. They're called unspoken rules."

Little Me: "Well, if it was unspoken, people shouldn't get mad at me for not knowing it."

Me: "Yeah, they shouldn't. But I'm pretty sure he wasn't as mad as he sounded. He just wanted you to stop right away."

Little Me: "I think he was mad. I think he doesn't like me."

Me: "He doesn't understand you, so he doesn't know how much you care about understanding the reasons for things."

Little Me: "Unspoken reasons?"

Me: "Unspoken reasons for unspoken rules."

Little Me: "Those aren't fair."

Me: "They're not, but you'll get better at figuring them out over time. It's even kind of fun to find the patterns behind them."

Little Me: "Patterns?"

Me: "Like, anything that might hurt someone is usually a bad idea."

Little Me: "I know that already."

Me: "But there are a million ways to apply it. And no one has listed all of them."

Little Me:	"I could! That sounds fun."
Me:	"You could, but the list would never be finished. It's better to learn how people think. Most of them think in a different way than you do."
Little Me:	"I know."
Me:	"You mean you know that it's different. Someday, you'll learn how—and why."

1

Discovery

How I Found Out Who I Am

As a child, I could already tell that most people experienced life very differently than I did. However, I suspected that there might be a few whose experiences were closer to mine—or almost the same, if we found ourselves in identical situations.

Every once in a while I would spot a stranger, or sometimes a minor character in a movie or play, and imagine that she might be one of the humans who felt like me. I imagined us having similar motivations, reactions, memories, and perspectives.

I had a word for such people—a "Me." I would see them and think to myself, *I wonder if she's a Me.*

I eventually learned that it wasn't just my imagination. I really do see the world differently, and was trying to spot others who share my neurotype—that is, minds on the autism spectrum. I even labeled it correctly, since "autism" comes from the Greek word for "self." Once I knew where to look, I found that the world is full of people like me.

Finding My People

In my mid-twenties, I met a new group of friends who understood me in ways that no one else did. They seemed to ignore societal expectations of how a person should sit, talk, move, dress, and act, freeing me to do the same. They also actively appreciated parts of my personality that others found annoying, such as my drive to clarify precisely what I mean.

My unspoken attitude toward these friends was always: "These people are so incredibly cool. Everyone who can't see past their odd mannerisms is truly missing out." I confess that I had the audacity and snobbery to imagine that strangers who saw me with them would do a double take, wonder why someone as "normal" as me was enjoying their company, and maybe reconsider their own prejudices. But I was more like my friends than I suspected.

A few years later, while visiting with these friends, the topic of utopias came up. One of them said that her idea of a utopia would be to live on a separate planet with all the people who are easy for her to talk to, and none of the people who aren't. I eagerly agreed, since I love her clear and direct communication style, and would enjoy a world full of such people.

"So... would I get to be on your planet?" I asked, hoping that the answer would be yes.

"Yes, definitely!" she answered. Then she added, "Oh, and 'autistic' is a short way to describe the kind of people I mean."

"Wait, what?" I asked, feeling both confused and curious. I knew almost nothing about autism at the time, except that it sometimes causes children to rock back and forth.

She encouraged me to go online and read autistic perspectives, to see if I relate to descriptions of how it feels on the inside. First, I decided to try the reverse: I thought of who I relate to most—the character Jane Eyre—then searched to see if she might be autistic.

According to one academic paper, she absolutely is. That paper, by Julia Miele Rodas, was a wonderful introduction to the history of autism as well as its common traits. I learned that I have many of those traits, especially social and sensory ones.

Socially, autistic people often communicate in a way that seems awkward to people who are not autistic. We tend to interpret statements literally, sometimes missing the additional layers of meaning tucked into sarcasm or body language. This can lead to misunderstandings, which some of us try to prevent by making our own words as clear and direct as possible. No wonder one of my childhood nicknames was Little Miss Precise!

Autistic people also react differently to sensory input than the average "neurotypical" person—someone whose brain resembles the majority. Sights and sounds that prompt a neutral reaction from most people can make autistics feel especially good or unusually bad, if they catch our attention at all. I didn't immediately notice the ways in which sensory discomfort was chipping away at my well-being, but I did immediately relate to descriptions of sensory joy—the ecstasy that I feel from heavy bass, wicker rugs, matte books, and flickering firelight.

How Autistic?

As I continued to research autism, though, I found that I didn't resonate with many of its stereotypical traits. I began to think that I might be "half autistic," because:

◇   I didn't avoid eye contact, or lack expression in my face or voice.

◇   I didn't have narrow interests, also known as "special interests."

◇   I didn't move in unusual ways, also known as "stimming."

Everything changed when I began to read about autistic women and girls. Many of their experiences mirrored mine perfectly—especially in their expressions, interests, and movements.

Yes, I can make eye contact, and I can adjust my face and voice to reflect the emotions I'm feeling. But it all takes concentration, and sometimes I get it wrong—for example, making more eye contact than my listener finds comfortable. "Masking" is a word for the performative effort required to get it right, which makes it tiring for me to socialize. External pressure to mask can come in the form of direct advice or indirect scorn, which are more often targeted at little girls than at little boys who behave the same way.

At first glance, my interests seem to cover a wide range of topics—art, literature, psychology, and music, to name a few. But after reading enough anecdotes from autistic women, I realized that everything I find deeply exciting falls into one of two specific categories. One is phenomenology, which involves noticing and analyzing how various experiences feel from the inside, such as whether you think in words or in pictures. The other category is aesthetic tropes, or the sensory elements that accompany a predictable story, such as the characters, setting, and soundtrack of a fairytale. It can be hard to recognize something as a special interest—a passion so strong that it counts as an autistic symptom—if it's as hard to label as mine are, or if it's a common interest that you approach with an uncommon passion.

If you met me in my early twenties, after I had some practice with masking and before I learned about autism, you might say that I moved in fairly typical ways. But that doesn't mean it came naturally. As I learned about the repetitive movements that autistic people use to calm anxiety, I realized that I was often suppressing such movements to avoid looking weird. If I entered a place where it felt socially acceptable, like if music was playing, then I was moving more than anyone. I also learned that tiny movements, such as fidgeting with a pen, count as stimming because they provide sensory stimulation.

Little by little, I came to realize that I must be fully autistic. What a significant discovery! It explained nearly every problem I'd had in life, as well as many of my quirks and talents. It was like learning for the first time that I'm actually an elf or mermaid or fairy—moreover, that there's nothing wrong with that, and that there are others like me.

It also opened the door to a whole new world of information, making my life so much easier. I found that I'm not alone in the challenges I face, and that other autistics have found solutions to many of those same challenges. I saw that by understanding my limits, I can find strategies to work within them—and by understanding my unique abilities, like precision and sensitivity, I can make the most of them.

If Only

How did it take me almost thirty years to even consider the possibility that there's a neurological reason for my differences? The clues were all there, but I wrote them off for various reasons. Sure, I had trouble with a lot of things—but so does everyone. I assumed that my autistic struggles were basic human struggles.

I thought communication was hard because I'm awkward and annoying. It's actually hard because I put extraordinary effort into processing and analyzing words, meanwhile missing the hidden meanings in gestures and tone. Maybe I could have grasped social expectations better if I'd asked more questions. Maybe others could have understood me better, including why I didn't meet their expectations, if I'd recognized and explained my differences.

I did notice that I often felt off-balance and in need of a hug, but I didn't make the connection to sensory overload. I could have done more to protect myself from feeling overwhelmed if I hadn't assumed my sensitivity was unreasonable. I also could have used stimming more strategically if I'd recognized its utility for self-calming.

On top of all that, I didn't realize how my attention to detail, both sensory and linguistic, can make it harder to see the big picture. This weakens my ability to plan and make decisions, and I get burnt out when I try to compensate with willpower. I could have learned methods to stay on track with daily habits, and also handled other responsibilities better, if I hadn't taken so long to recognize my need for external systems.

If I could go back in time, would I tell Little Me about the word "autism"? Not unless I could also explain what that means, since the resources available to learn about autism back then were sparse and often misleading. But since a multitude of useful information has been written by actual autistics in the past ten years, I wish every autistic person today would learn the term and feel comfortable using it.

Diagnosis

After I became certain that I'm autistic, I felt driven to share everything I was learning—both to help the people in my life understand me better, and to help other autistics understand themselves. I started with face-to-face conversations. Some people were skeptical of my autism at first, since I don't fit some of the stereotypes. But most came to accept it after I spent enough time explaining—sometimes an hour or more.

I thought that a diagnosis might help reduce the time it takes to prove I'm autistic, so I began looking for a psychologist to evaluate me for autism. I spent some time researching and phoning local psychologists, but I couldn't find one who had ever diagnosed an adult woman with autism. Finally, through word of mouth, I found one who was sixty miles away, and I booked an evaluation there.

It took many hours, spread across three appointments. There were also forms for me to fill out at home, and other forms for my parents to fill out about me. Additionally, I got the idea to write a comprehensive list of every autistic trait I could identify in myself—six single-spaced pages, organized according to the symptoms of autism listed in *The Diagnostic and Statistical Manual of Mental Disorders* (or "the DSM" for short). One item on my list was the need to make lists!

When the evaluation was complete and the psychologist finally revealed the result, I threw my hands up in celebration. It was an official confirmation of the truth I already knew—I am, indeed, autistic!

Self-Diagnosis

Many people believe they're autistic, and are accepted as such by other autistics, but have trouble getting a diagnosis, because they don't match the narrow criteria in the DSM. A diagnosis is useful for requesting accommodations—a word that schools and companies use for extra support or modified requirements—so it can be worth the trouble for that reason alone. But if, like me, your main reason is to convince doubters, a diagnosis may or may not help with that.

If you identify as autistic, people may doubt it because you don't "look autistic." If you identify as autistic, and you spend enough time and effort to explain why, people may doubt it because you don't have the medical establishment's seal of approval. If you get officially diagnosed, and it happens easily, people may doubt it because they believe the process wasn't thorough enough to be accurate, and it's becoming too easy for anyone to get a diagnosis these days. If you get officially diagnosed, and it happens through blood, sweat, tears, and red tape—through an arduous and complex process involving your doctor, your family, and in some cases your school—even then, people may still doubt it.

At some point, enough is enough. At some point, you have to abandon the urge to justify yourself further, because it's a moving target. If you find comfort and joy in the same things that give autistic people comfort and joy, then no one can take that away.

Besides, the diagnostic criteria for autism are based on a list of observable behaviors. The more I've learned about these seemingly unrelated traits, the more I've realized that what makes me autistic is not my outer actions, but the inner neurology that produces them.

2

Unpuzzling

How Autism Works

One of my earliest introductions to autism was a bumper sticker that said, "My autistic kid rocks—colloquially and kinesthetically!" That was accurate, but incomplete. It took me a while to learn that although rocking is a visible action, autism itself is an internal state that causes different actions in different people.

Does it have external effects? Sure—in how I move, speak, react, and position my body. But if you took away all of that, my mind would still be autistic. No matter how I appear on the outside, I will always be autistic on the inside.

However, that's a relatively new way to think about autism. Historically, in the DSM, autism has been defined by a list of behaviors. On closer examination, most of those are traits that a certain kind of mind exhibits under distress.

I find it useful to have a term for that kind of mind, so I'm happy that more people are starting to use the term "autism" for a neurotype with a cluster of predispositions. From birth, it makes some things enjoyable and other things hard. It makes a person more vulnerable to experiencing certain kinds of distress, but doesn't guarantee that will happen.

I also think it's useful to have a term for the way this particular neurotype interacts with stressors. The DSM calls it "autism spectrum disorder" (ASD), but I prefer to call it "autistic distress." It varies over time, based on the environment and the intensity of any co-occurring conditions. So, a person might qualify for a diagnosis of ASD at some points in life but not others, while remaining consistently autistic.

Using the word "autism" for both concepts (a neurotype and its response to stress) has created a lot of confusion, a lot of stigma, and a lot of missed opportunities for support. Both are accurate descriptors of me, but when I say that I'm autistic, I'm generally referring to autism as a neurotype.

Theories of Autism

Seeing autism as a neurotype helps to explain why it has a unique effect on each person. But why does autism create such a wide spectrum of traits?

Autistic people process information differently, because our brains are hyper-connected in some places and less connected in others. This difference is visible on brain scans—we have neural pathways that others don't, like secret passages all over our brains. This results in a torrent of information for each of us to process, including physical sensations and pattern recognition. By default, everything is intense, which has been called "Intense World Theory."

We survive by filtering some parts out. It's as if every form of input has a volume knob, and ours are all the way up by default—so we turn some down to compensate, but can't control which ones. And here's what creates the variety: Different people filter out different kinds of information. Then, what we don't filter out becomes our focus. It's comforting, and often necessary, to drown out the noise by turning all of our attention to one thing at a time, which has been called "Monotropism."

With such intense focus, we often miss clues about what will happen next in our environment and interactions. Thus, a lot of autistic distress comes from living in a state of constant surprise. This is one application of "Predictive Coding Theory," also known as "Predictive Processing Theory."

Any of these theories, alone or together, can explain the variety of traits that we label as autism. It affects our social interactions, communication, relationships, physical movements, habits, interests, and sensory experiences—all of which are mentioned in the DSM. However, autism can cause additional effects beyond what the DSM describes, especially when it intersects with co-occurring conditions. There's a kaleidoscope of ways to be autistic, and that's why we call it a spectrum.

Where Attention Goes

An autistic brain structure could theoretically draw a person's attention to anything, but there are some common patterns. Autistic people tend to notice spoken language more than body language and tone. Most of us notice surprising sights and sounds more than consistent ones, and pay more attention to sensory input in general than the average person does.

Everything else about autism is downstream from this. We often miss social cues, because we take people literally. We often move in a rhythm, because it soothes our overstimulated senses. We often experience anxiety, and sometimes even trauma, from sensory shock and unexplained rejection. We often turn to predictable foods, objects, phrases, and interests, because they shield our bodies from shock and our minds from mystery.

Some autistics, in some circumstances, can learn to notice some of the things we naturally ignore. But it's easy for non-autistics to forget that we aren't just replacing one focus of attention with another. Rather, we're adding more kinds of information on top of what we naturally notice.

That can feel incredibly overwhelming. Meltdowns and shutdowns, which are often considered symptoms of autism, can result from the strain of pulling our attention in too many directions.

Unpuzzling My Life

Understanding how autism works, beyond just the DSM criteria, helped me to see my past in a new light—especially high school, where I felt that everyone perceived me as annoying and weird.

I was always pointing out everyone's mistakes, including any words that teachers spelled wrong on the whiteboard.

I was always clueless about social drama. There would be cliques, and rumors, and classmates mad at one another for some reason— and I would never pick up on any of it.

I was always raising my hand and asking a ton of questions. Many times, teachers would say, "We went over this already!" But there was usually some part that I still didn't understand.

I was always climbing random objects. I'd be up on a ledge, or a rafter, or the top shelf of a closet—unexpected places, accidentally surprising anyone who happened to spot me.

I didn't exactly fit in, but I turned out fine. Over time, I began to notice silver linings behind my mysterious behaviors, even if their unifying cause remained clouded.

In high school, noticing errors made me unpopular. Later, rising through the ranks of a marketing and web development company, it became my job to ensure that everyone else's work was technically correct.

In high school, gossip went over my head. Now, I have wonderful, deep friendships with people who are kind, and who value my kindness, as well as my sincerity.

In high school, I needed clear explanations with precise detail. Now, as a writer, I can give other people such explanations, which helps them to understand what they didn't before.

In high school, I wanted to be up on top of every obstacle. Now, having trained in parkour for ten years, I've learned to surmount higher and higher obstacles.

Nevertheless, in spite of all this, I still had a lingering sense that to some people, I would always be seen as annoying and weird. That's why it was incredibly affirming to learn the root cause of all my quirks. Autism gave me a more complete, more accurate self-image than the unflattering labels that I previously believed.

Why do errors jump out at me? Because autistic people often notice tiny details. We catch things that other people miss.

Why does drama go over my head? Because autistic people also miss things that other people catch. When we hear a person say something that's different from what they actually mean, we tend to take it at face value.

Why am I so precise and literal? Because autistic people deal with so much misunderstanding and miscommunication in areas that aren't clearly defined, like tone. So when something is possible for me to clarify—like a homework assignment, or my own motives—then I feel driven to do so.

Why do I feel drawn to places that are high up, separate from everyone else? Because autistic people take in so much sensory information that everything seems louder and brighter and more overwhelming to us. I like to tuck myself away in a corner, because it gives me some safety for my senses.

All of this explains why I struggle a lot in some situations, and do very well in others. I don't do well with big-picture planning, but I'm great at zeroing in on the details. I don't do well around social drama, but I'm great around people who say what they mean. I don't do well with vague instructions, but I'm great at following a process when I know all the steps. I don't do well in noisy crowds, but I'm great in small groups or one-on-one.

Disability or Superpower?

I believe that autism can be a superpower, because it means perceiving an abundance of sensory details and patterns. Some things are overwhelmingly beautiful. I also believe that autism can be a disability, because it means struggling to process all that information. Some things are just plain overwhelming.

I know that some autistic people dislike calling it a superpower, because that creates pressure to display savant skills that they may not have. I also know that some people—autistic and otherwise—prefer not to think of it as a disability, due to negative connotations of that term. I'm grateful that those connotations have recently been shifting in a more positive direction, thanks to advocates who are proud of their disabilities.

I personally see autism as a superpower, a disability, or a combination of both, depending on the situation. It's like being a mermaid who can navigate vast waters, but sometimes finds herself stuck on dry land.

However, my favorite way to think of autism is this: *I miss what others catch, and I catch what others miss.* If you read the rest of this book through that lens, you may be able to see what I've caught or missed that has led to each experience I describe—keeping in mind that other autistic people may catch or miss different things than I do.

3

Sensitivity

How It Feels to Feel So Much

I hardly ever feel completely at ease in my body. Usually, something is too cold or too hot, too wobbly or too firm, too tight or too loose—it's very rare for everything to feel just right.

But then there are moments when the outdoor air is exactly as warm as my skin, turning the sunshine into an embrace and the breeze into a caress, and in those moments I believe that bodies must be the most marvelous invention in history.

Overall, it's as if I was born into a fairytale, with a fairy who came to my christening and told everyone, "She will feel everything!" Would that be a good gift? Yes, and no, and sometimes both at once.

Sensory Beauty

Sensory sensitivity is a wonderful gift when it causes me to appreciate beauty.

I once read a blog post by a mother who was mourning her son's autism. One of her main complaints was that all he wanted to do all day was stare out the window at trees.

On reading that, my reaction was to applaud the child's aesthetic taste, approve of how he spends his time, and wish I could afford to do the same. Why? Well, trees are incredible. It's something about the way sunlight filters through leaves as they dance on the wind—ever changing yet intuitively predictable, captivating yet calming.

As a child, I loved climbing trees. As an adult, I can do more than climb them. A few summers ago, I rented a treehouse for a weekend. Soon after, I was commissioned to create a series of tree paintings!

Maybe that boy will grow up to do even greater things. Maybe not. In any case, I sincerely hope that his family will one day begin to see what he sees.

Sensory Pain

Sensory sensitivity is challenging when it causes me pain, though. For example, I'm so sensitive to water that raindrops feel like I'm being poked with a pencil.

Before I found out that I take in more sensory data than most people, I wasn't able to explain how water affects me. My inner narrative didn't include the observation that rain hurts my skin, because every time I flinched at it, people would say, "It won't hurt you!"

For someone with sensory sensitivity, who takes things literally, this is confusing and unhelpful to hear. It's also inaccurate. What they really meant was that it won't *harm* me. But because I took them literally, I never thought to label the feeling as pain.

Normally, when something hurts you, it causes you to stop and think about how much danger you're in. A papercut may hurt a lot, but when you realize it's just a papercut, you know you'll be okay.

It's hard to do this without first recognizing the feeling. When I began to accept that water does hurt me, I was able to realize that it won't harm me, and that the pain I feel is disproportionate to the actual danger. Knowing this, I have a bit more courage to face the rain—but I also feel less silly putting up an umbrella when I need to.

I think it's important to trust the words that people use to describe how they feel, but also to notice what they're communicating through behavior. If someone had trusted that my reactions to rain were reasonable, I might have trusted myself a lot sooner, too.

Beauty and Pain

Sometimes, sensory delight can outweigh sensory pain. Water becomes less of a problem for me when there's more of it, like when I'm swimming in an ocean.

It feels so good, deep in my bones, to move myself through the otherworldly substance, buoyed up by the rhythm of waves or propelled forward in exhilaration as they crash. Yet it feels so terrible when wet skin meets the air, and trickling droplets transform into sharp pricks by the slightest breath of wind.

I wish that I could be in water without water being on me. But some kinds of heaven are worth going through hell, and water can be both.

Sensory Value

Even after learning how strong my senses are, it took me a while to see the value of indulging them. A turning point was when my friend Alex asked if I wanted to see his notebook collection. I readily agreed, because notebooks are portals of possibility that cause my imagination to soar.

I was not disappointed. Crowning a corner bookcase, like an altar, was a neat row of spines. Perusing each one, leafing through its bare pages, felt like touching the ground from which a wondrous story might grow.

"Do you have any plans for them?" I asked. "Ideas for what to write?"

"No," he answered. "I just like them."

What? I thought. *You can just do that? You can keep something simply because you like it, free from any pressure to use it for a particular purpose?*

I wish I had learned earlier in life that it's okay to enjoy things for sensory reasons alone. As a kid, I played with different toys for different reasons. Some were fun because I could use them to act out my favorite stories. Others were fun for visual or tactile reasons—I liked how they looked, or how they felt in my hand.

But I didn't notice the difference. I only knew which toys were fun, and didn't think much about why. Instead, for some reason, I believed that toys were only worth keeping if I could use them in a story. For example, I had some squishy foam blocks that I used as beds for my Barbie dolls. When I no longer enjoyed playing with Barbie dolls, I got rid of the blocks... and now regret it.

No one told me that it's fine to keep things just because they feel nice. No one told me that it's perfectly acceptable, even as an adult, to line up a row of soft blocks and push down on each one, feeling it flatten and watching it rise again, as a calming break from a chaotic world. No one told me, because I never asked. I just assumed it wasn't okay, because it wasn't what other people did.

I've grown better at accepting what I enjoy. First, though, I had to get better at noticing what I enjoy, and why. Now, I've got a collection of objects that I enjoy for sensory reasons alone—including some pristine notebooks that I intend to keep that way.

Sensory Discomfort

It also took me a while to notice what I don't enjoy, and begin taking action to avoid it. Not only does water hurt my skin, but sudden noises also hurt my ears, fluorescent light hurts my eyes, and cold wind hurts my neck. Yet somehow, I spent years believing that life is just uncomfortable by default, and trying to muffle that with happy and meaningful activities—not seeing that I could also tackle the discomfort at its source.

Tomato seeds are one example of a sensory experience that I don't find painful, but do find terribly unpleasant. It isn't that I mind the seeds themselves, but the gunk surrounding them is disgusting to me, like phlegm. As a child, I always wanted to scoop out the gunk. But I never did so, because it felt wasteful to discard something that everyone else treated as food.

I vowed to myself that when I grew up, and was able to buy my own tomatoes with my own money, I would remove all the gross parts and only eat the thick, red, juicy parts. The first time I did so, it felt like a coming of age. It meant so much more to me than just a tasty tomato—it symbolized the freedom to act on my own sensory preferences.

The thing is, I probably had more of that freedom as a child than I realized. If I'd explained how much I disliked tomato seeds, I'm sure my parents would have let me remove them. But little autistic girls are often more conscientious than other kids about doing what's expected, so I never considered that possibility.

A benefit of avoiding sensory distress is that it increases my ability to handle everything else. When a situation gets easier on a sensory level, it gets easier on an intellectual level too.

I first noticed this principle when my grocery store updated its shopping carts. Unlike the old carts, the new ones go smoothly and silently around corners, like a fish swiveling around a maze of coral. Without the distraction of forceful turns and clanking wheels—which I can feel through my hands, even with headphones or earplugs—I found that I was able to make decisions much faster.

Sensory Protection

I sometimes feel driven to protect my senses without even realizing it. I'm getting better at paying attention to those instincts, but they often seem odd at first.

Whenever I worry that I'm being ridiculous, my boyfriend Jake has a talent for helping me identify the valid logic that subconsciously drives my actions. Like, I felt silly after packing twelve pairs of socks for a three-day trip, though he didn't see any problem with it. He reminded me that there's no sock police, but I needed to understand my motivation before I could accept it.

After discussing it, we uncovered the fact that my motivation was sensory—I didn't know which length and weight of socks the weather would require each day, and the wrong kind would have made me uncomfortable. To prevent that, I needed four pairs per day. But, as I pointed out, that goes against the common advice to pack one pair of socks for each day of a trip, and a couple of spares just in case.

He compared that advice to mass-produced clothing—it fits most people reasonably well, and some people terribly. I try to remember that, especially when my gut seems to go against common sense. It's not that I always go with my gut, but at least I respect its potential wisdom and try to understand it.

Sensory Empathy

In addition to making my own life more intense, sensory sensitivity affects how I relate to others. I sometimes struggle to predict how words will make people feel, but I have a visceral reaction when I witness them reacting to sensory input.

I empathize very strongly whenever I hear the sound of a crying child, especially a wailing baby. It seems to me like a very reasonable reaction to the frequent frustrations of daily life, and I feel as if they're speaking on my behalf with sounds that aren't socially acceptable for me to make.

There is a myth that autistic people lack empathy. Maybe it's because we can't always tell how people feel from their facial expressions alone. Or maybe it's because we often express empathy in different ways than they would. Sensory empathy, in particular, may sometimes be too intense for us to process and put into words.

Deeply feeling what others feel is, I believe, one of the greatest gifts autistic people have to offer the world. When others are in pain and I feel it too, it comforts me to remember that such empathy is a beautiful thing, because it moves me to help. The same emotion that feels like weakness may someday alert me to someone's deep need. This hopefulness and purpose make it easier for me to bear someone's pain in moments when I can do nothing to help.

I also try to remind myself that whatever they're going through, it will get better. They will survive. And so will I, on days when I feel the same way.

4

Processing

How I Take It All In

Processing speed is different from processing ability. Sometimes, when a person realizes I have poor processing speed, they automatically assume I have poor processing ability. Their tone becomes more lilting, their vocabulary more childlike, and their expressions more performative, as if they think any of that will make it easier for me to understand them. It's like they've never considered the possibility that a person can be both smart and slow.

I can't handle a barrage of facts, descending haphazardly into my mind like Tetris. I freeze up, game over. However, I can handle extremely complex information if you give it to me one bite at a time, with pauses in between to digest each new fact.

Everyone deserves respect, regardless of processing speed or ability. But those are separate needs with separate accommodations, and they don't always overlap.

Processing Audio

I process all information slower than average, but especially audio.

Because it's more of a delay than a lack of ability, it took me years to figure out that there was anything different about my experience.

My first clue was noticing that I procrastinate listening to any audio or video clips that people send me, sometimes even splitting the task across multiple days. Once I realized how much easier I find reading, I started going right to the transcript each time. If there isn't one, I ask for a summary instead.

This is self-advocacy. It doesn't always mean saying that I'm autistic. Sometimes I simply brainstorm, *What would make this about as easy for me as for a typical person?* and then ask for that. However, if I haven't disclosed that I'm autistic—and sometimes even if I have—I can't necessarily count on others to understand my need for assistance or alternatives.

I find that this lack of empathy is more common with phone calls than with audio recordings. People often say, "Just pick up the phone, it's so much more efficient!" It's true that phone calls are more efficient if you measure from dialing to hanging up, since most people don't reply immediately to emails. But phone calls take longer for me overall, if you include all my steps before and after the call:

◇ Write down what I plan to say, usually as bullet points but sometimes as full sentences.

◇ Plan a flow chart of additional things I might need to say, depending on how the call goes.

◇ Breathe deeply to gather courage.

◇ Make the call, reading my notes aloud.

◇ Write down any important information I learn, as well as any follow-up steps I need to take.

◇ Take some time to recover and collect my thoughts, until I'm able to focus on other things again.

Making an official call, for example to book an appointment or get technical support, requires all of these steps. When calling a friend, I can usually skip some of them. But emailing only requires the first step, so I'm grateful to live at a time in history when the Internet exists. It gives me a way to communicate that's more enjoyable, and also more efficient for me, if people are willing to use it.

Processing Transitions

Besides audio, transitions are the biggest challenge for me to process. When someone teaches me a new skill, I usually ask them to go slowly from each step to the next. Historically, this has helped me to stay calm amid an onslaught of new information. However, what helps even more is a pause at every transition, with the opportunity to decide when I'm ready to keep going. Sometimes, I'm ready immediately. Other times, I have clarifying questions. Most times, I need a moment to figure out how I feel.

I also need time to transition between places. Whenever I drive to a place where I'll need to be social, I spend a few minutes alone in my parked car before I go in. I spend this time shifting my expectations from the safety of solitude to the possibility of surprises.

Even if there's no need to leave the house, I still hardly get anything done for half a day before a scheduled call or visit. Part of me feels like I'm giving in to an illusion—the idea that an item on the calendar casts a spell of uselessness on the preceding hours. But that tendency is meeting a real need, as I discovered one day when I tried to fight it. Before a video call, I only spent twenty minutes getting ready—both logistically (gathering what I needed) and mentally (imagining how it would begin). Until the twenty-minute mark, I kept crossing things off my to-do list and ignoring the upcoming call.

At the start of the call, I felt very dysregulated. For me, that looks like breathing harder, bouncing from thought to thought with the constant sense that I'm forgetting something, and feeling like my body is floating insecurely through space. It's because twenty minutes of preparation wasn't enough—not for me, anyway.

The more years I spend exploring my brain and analyzing my challenges, the more I realize the vital importance and wide-ranging benefits of this one simple accommodation: Time.

Cognitive Overload

When I don't have enough time to process or prepare, and my attempts to self-advocate fall flat, my brain begins to feel so full that there's no room left for new thoughts or actions. I call this "cognitive overload," and I find it harder to describe than any other experience. Regardless of whether I notice it in the moment or replay it later in my imagination, it's so all-consuming that it pushes out the possibility of analytical observation.

By itself, cognitive overload is not distressing to me. What causes distress is any little thing added on top—such as a question, a change in my environment, or a required action. I suppose you could say that cognitive overload is like a load on a camel's back. My number one priority, in that state, is to avoid adding any new straws.

Trouble with Speech

An overloaded brain makes it harder to talk. Even ordinary, daily stressors can add up to the point where something has to give, and that something is fluent speech.

That happened to me once in a staff meeting over Zoom. I used the chat box to ask a question, since I always find typing easier than talking, but especially when I've had a hard day. Someone asked me to clarify what I meant, and I thought I could do it verbally, but the words sputtered out in a cumbersome order.

Later that day, I needed to make a phone call, but I kept bursting into tears every time I tried to dial. I decided not to cancel a visit with Jake that evening, but brought along a whiteboard to share my thoughts. He encourages me to do that whenever I need to, as well as any time I would simply prefer it.

This is what it's like to have fluctuating abilities. My autism diagnosis states that I'm "without verbal impairment," because that's true 99% of the time. But once every hundred days or so, I get a day where talking is a hundred times harder.

The very hardest time for me to talk is when I'm startled. If a sudden noise hurts my ears, and a stranger asks if I'm okay, I silently think, *I'm not okay. You've caught me off-guard, only halfway recovered from an overwhelming moment. I'm trying to regain my sense of balance, as if I was spinning and suddenly stopped. Finding words right now feels like dizzily trying to find which way is up, although every wordless moment increases the tension between us. But when you ask if I'm okay, all you really want to know is if I'll be okay without help.*

"Yeah," I try to say aloud. It takes strength to spit out that one syllable, and I usually get it out on the second or third attempt. I may not be fully okay at that point, but I know I will be soon.

Asking for Time

I like being polite. But it becomes harder when information comes at me too fast to keep up. My brain panics a little, like I've been pushed out of a tree and am grasping for branches as I fall.

Once, a colleague started asking me a detailed question without any context. I wish I'd said, "Sorry, I need some background info first. Can you please explain the purpose of what you're trying to do?"

Instead, I curtly interrupted, "Wait—back up—context!"

In the rush of the moment, I can't always find the right words. But if I figure out a script ahead of time, I can usually follow it. My life is full of situations where I react awkwardly, prepare a script, and do better the next time.

That day, I figured out that whenever I feel overwhelmed by a complex question, I should respond, "Sorry, I need..." By the time I get those words out, I may know exactly what I need. If I don't, then my next words can be: "A moment to think."

I was able to recognize my needs at a medical appointment when the doctor informed me that my blood pressure was higher than the previous time. "That's because you were asking me questions as you tested it," I answered, "and multitasking is stressful. Can you try again?"

She retested it, this time in silence except for instructions about the testing. My blood pressure was fine. That appointment broke a myth I'd previously believed—that asking for more time is inefficient. If it saves repetition, it's actually more efficient.

When I try to do too much at once, it makes me anxious. If I notice the anxiety soon enough, I can follow one of my scripts, such as:

◇ "I just need a moment to finish this first."

◇ "I'll answer as soon as this is done."

◇ "I can't do both things at once."

If I notice the anxiety too late, though, I lose the ability to articulate what I need. My brain goes into overdrive, and my mouth can't find a way to explain it.

Writing Is Easier

Even when it's possible for me to talk fluently, I still process ideas much better through writing. Talking feels messy, but writing clarifies and crystallizes all my thoughts and feelings. I especially benefit from making a list, any sort of list—a history of what happened, a plan for next steps, or simply an inventory of the thoughts taking up space in my brain. If I see my ideas in text form, it's easier to organize and remember them, as well as notice connections.

When I'm writing, I often ramble a bit before stumbling on the main idea. I might delete the first half of a draft, move the last sentence to the beginning, and make other adjustments before finally sharing it. Now, imagine what that sounds like when I try to do it verbally, in real time. It can seem like I'm jumping all over the place! But it doesn't feel that way. From the inside, it feels like one coherent idea—an idea that I'm refining, expanding, and improving.

It feels good to summarize my thoughts after untangling them, like taking a snapshot of a finished puzzle. When I do, some people react with frustration: "You already said that!" Others react with relief: "You lost me for a minute, but now it all makes sense." I never know which reaction I'll get, so I prefer to write.

When All Goes Well

Jake says that he imagines the inside of my brain like the interior of a Gothic castle. In its grandest room, stained glass windows stretch all the way up the walls, spilling colorful light onto rows of desks where scribes sit typing. What they write gets sent up pneumatic tubes, to be archived in the lofty towers.

This scene, part medieval and part steampunk, really resonates with my internal experience of processing information. Sometimes it gets backed up, with a flurry of paperwork spilling all over the floor, and the sound of typewriters clattering furiously. Other times it's neat and orderly, with everything properly recorded and sent to a perfect place for future retrieval.

Information can be sensory or social, visual or verbal, absorbing the present moment or assessing future possibilities. All of it has to go through some sort of processing before I'm able to act on it. But with enough external calm, and enough time to think, my mind is a very pleasant place to be.

5

Stimming

How I Let It All Out

"How are you doing?" I asked a possibly autistic colleague, curious how she was feeling about new responsibilities at work.

She flapped her arms in classic autistic fashion, her face looking overwhelmed but full of hopeful determination. She reminded me of a baby bird trying to make it out of the nest, or a fish trying to swim upstream.

"Staying afloat," she said. "It's just... I'm staying afloat."

And I thought, how beautiful—that's what we're all doing, all the autistics who flap. When we could so easily sink under the weight of our senses, the complexity of our thoughts, the expectations of others, and the wonder of the universe... we flap, and it keeps us afloat.

I enjoyed flapping long before I knew what it was called. In middle school, my classmates and I created an air band—like air guitar, but with other instruments too. At lunchtime, we would put on a CD and each pretend to play an instrument. I was always on the drums, hitting invisible rhythms with invisible drumsticks, and it felt like the most natural thing in the world.

I didn't realize at the time that I was essentially flapping. I didn't know I was autistic, but my sliver of social awareness was enough to recognize that in most contexts, most people don't flap.

The invisible band gave me a socially acceptable space for an action that felt really good to my body and brain. I wish the whole world could be like that for autistics. In the meantime, we need more spaces like that—spaces to be free.

How Stimming Helps

Flapping is just one of many ways to "stim," or meet a natural need for sensory stimulation, but there are many more. Rocking, humming, rubbing, and bouncing are other excellent ways to release the stress of an intense moment. I self-censored thousands of times throughout my life before realizing that the best way for me to handle strong emotions is to transform them into something else, such as movement.

Emotions can feel like a physical force, welling up in my chest and bursting out through my limbs, so rocking or swaying gives them a place to go. My friend Robby once observed, "You can't contain all the happiness in one place, so you have to distribute it across space." That's true for both positive and negative emotions.

I remember reading an adventure novel as a child, and pausing right at the climax to run around the couch, because I just couldn't take the excitement. The pressure under my feet gave me "proprioceptive input," and the circular movement gave me "vestibular input," which together helped me settle down enough to finish the book.

When an emotion is too deep for movement and too complex for words, it comes out in sounds—squealing with excitement, groaning with discomfort, sighing with contentment. Vocal stimming is harder for me to control than movement, but also more rare.

Compression

Another great source of sensory stimulation, one that isn't based in movement or sound, is compression. When I'm not getting enough of it, my whole world feels off-balance. Weighted blankets help, and so does rolling on the floor, but nothing quite compares to a long, tight hug. Here is how it feels to need a hug, and then to get one:

◇ My self spills out of my body in every direction, like a punctured barrel. A hug plugs up the holes, keeping me intact.

◇ My thoughts swarm around my head, fuzzy and uncatchable. A hug gathers them up, pauses their motion, and sets them down where I can see them.

◇ My arms don't know where they want to be. Any position I take feels awkward and wrong. A hug slides me back into place, snugly fitting into my own existence.

There are many problems that can't be solved by a hug. But it has a huge, immediate impact when I'm in a particular state of body and mind, craving compression.

Overstimulated vs. Understimulated

The desire for a hug or other sensory input can arise because of too little stimulation—or too much. Stimming while overstimulated might sound counterintuitive, but it helps because it's repetitive and predictable. Like a white noise machine for the body, it drowns out other input and makes me feel more grounded.

A key feature of autism, which distinguishes it from similar neurotypes, is the tendency to waver between overstimulation and understimulation, depending on the environment and the day. Sometimes I even feel both at once, in different parts of my body, and it can be all-consuming to figure out what's happening inside me and what to do about it. At those times, it's nice that stimming helps with both overstimulation and understimulation.

Self-soothing

Stimming isn't just for autistics. Many people pace or twirl their hair, with a similarly soothing effect. But autistics tend to do it more often, to combat the frequent stresses we face. I think that we make better use of stimming than most people do, but everyone could benefit from strategies for self-soothing. So whether you're autistic or not, here are some ideas that might feel surprisingly good:

◇ **Rocking:** Play a song that you enjoy, something that usually makes you sway from side to side. This time, though, try swaying forward and backward.

◇ **Compression:** If you can, ask someone you love to hug you tightly for a whole minute. If you can't, make a pile of every blanket you own and then crawl underneath.

◇ **Textures:** Close your eyes, reach into your closet, and touch various pieces of clothing until you find one that feels extra nice, or at least extra interesting. Stroke it gently, really noticing how it feels.

◇ **Flapping:** Next time you wash your hands, shake them off instead of using a towel. Try side to side, up and down, round in circles, or all over the place.

Regardless of whether any of these ideas become a regular habit, experiencing the sensation from the inside may at least help you to empathize with why autistic people stim.

Risks of Stimming

What if you find that you're seeking stimulation by doing something harmful, like hitting or scratching? I think the best approach is to look for another action that's equally satisfying, which usually requires a lot of experimenting. Keep in mind that experimentation is easier to do when calm, since some ideas won't work, and in moments of stress it feels urgent to use something that works.

However, self-harm isn't the only risk of stimming. I've spent most of my life fighting what my body needs, because I know that if I give in, people might perceive me as a threat. For example:

◇ **Percussive movement**, such as stomping my feet or whacking my palms on my thighs, could seem threatening because it looks like violence.

◇ **Sudden movement**, such as stretching out my arms and fingers after curling them up just moments before, could seem threatening if it startles people.

◇ **Facial movement**, such as wrinkling my nose or squeezing my eyes shut, could seem threatening because it makes my thoughts and feelings appear mysterious at best, and offensive at worst.

◇ **Childlike movement**, such as swaying or flapping, could seem threatening because overt playfulness in grown-up movie characters is often used as a signal of insanity.

In public, I tend to mask my most unusual movements. In private, I'd prefer to drop the mask, but I find it surprisingly difficult. I don't have an easy way to toggle between battle and surrender, control and acceptance, vigilance and ease.

For example, when I'm lying awake at night, I sometimes get a strong urge to rub my feet together like a cricket—so I do. But before learning about stimming, I always paused partway through, just to prove I could. For some reason, I thought the behavior was acceptable if I could stop it, and not if I couldn't. I sensed a stigma around letting such a seemingly useless action master me—no matter how good it felt, how necessary, how powerfully cathartic, or how harmless.

But it isn't useless. It's a way to self-regulate, or get into a frame of mind where self-control is easier. So in the end, stimming doesn't take away control—it gives it.

Approaches to Stimming

Stimming can sometimes be risky, or at least disruptive, depending on the context. But if I don't let my feelings out, they build up inside. So in situations when it's safe to stim, I try to take full advantage of it—not just reactively, but also proactively. The evolution of my approach to stimming went something like this:

◇ **Bad:** *I shouldn't let myself stim.*

◇ **Good:** *I should let myself stim when I feel like it.*

◇ **Better:** *I should remember, when I'm anxious or overwhelmed, that stimming is a strategy I can intentionally use to calm myself.*

◇ **Best:** *I should remember, when I'm about to enter a stressful situation, that stimming is a strategy I can use to prepare myself ahead of time.*

In addition to stimming proactively, I'm also trying to pay attention to any urges I get to move in unconventional ways. Sometimes I might react to them, and sometimes not, but at least I want to notice them.

One day, as Jake was telling a complex story, I noticed that I was imagining all the nouns in the story as invisible blocks floating in front of me. I felt an urge to reach out and arrange them according to the unfolding plot of the story, because I remember things better when I can connect them to a position in space.

I interrupted briefly, to explain what I was about to do. He already knows that I'm trying to let myself move more freely, but this kind of meaningful movement was a new idea.

"So you're just, like, a little bundle of constrained interpretive dance?" he asked with a smile.

It's true, I am—even more than he realized. Years before we met, I used to dance all the time, especially styles of dance that reflect the lyrics of a song. I think it's because my body feels drawn to put everything into motion. Stimming is a way for me to let out feelings, but also ideas.

Feeling Just Right

My idea of a perfect moment is one that stimulates all of my senses at once—but gently, without surprises. A perfect balance is nearly impossible to plan, but occasionally it just happens.

My favorite example is sitting by a crackling fire, squished between friends on a couch, sipping hot tea, with someone softly playing acoustic guitar nearby. Bonus points if we're discussing one of my special interests too, to stimulate my mind.

This is a paradox of autism: Too much stimulation can make my nervous system feel dysregulated, but so can too little. At best, dysregulation feels like something is not right—like I was born for cozy fires with friends, and I'm not living my destiny. At worst, it can feel like my whole world is falling apart.

Moreover, this is a paradox of stimming: When I'm already overstimulated, stimming calms me by drowning out the harsh feelings with nice, predictable ones. And when I'm understimulated, it awakens my senses to focus and be present.

I wish there was a way to subtly stimulate all of my senses at once, whenever I needed. I wish I could use stimming to simulate that feeling by the fire, without any negative effects.

Skin Picking

Unfortunately, the one stim that comes closest to making me feel just right also causes the most problems: I find it very satisfying to pick at my skin. When I first heard about stimming, I didn't recognize all the ways I did it, until I read that skin picking is a stim—one that's particularly common for autistic women.

Extreme skin picking is officially called "dermatillomania" or "skin excoriation disorder." I don't struggle with the similar habit of extreme hair pulling, called "trichotillomania," but many of my observations about skin picking also apply to hair pulling, and might apply to other unwanted stims too.

The habits of skin picking and hair pulling meet multiple needs at once. They're like the Swiss Army knives of anxiety coping methods. If you want to stop, you probably won't be able to find a perfect replacement. Instead, you may have to use different tools for different kinds of needs:

◇ **Sensory needs** are the most obvious, since derma and trich are forms of stimming. Experiment with alternate stims, but don't limit yourself to ones that seem similar. I find compression surprisingly helpful, even though it doesn't imitate the "picking" motion.

◇ **Safety needs** are harder to notice. Try asking, "What am I afraid will happen if I leave this scab/flake/nail/hair alone?" Compliant children, in particular, may grow into adults who can't help feeling that things are "supposed" to be a certain way. Remember that beautiful trees have rough surfaces, and it's safe for you to have them too.

◇ **Cerebral needs** take at least two forms. If my mind is overstimulated, then picking can be a calming, meditative activity.

If my mind is understimulated, then picking can be a fascinating, exploratory activity. In the moment, I can't always tell which state I'm in. But if staring at a candle is helpful, then I was probably overstimulated, and if researching a special interest is helpful, then I was probably understimulated.

When I feel like picking at my skin, the best strategy I've found is to do one quick thing in each of these categories. If I can manage to do that without picking along the way, it usually relieves the urge. If it doesn't, I give in and pick. Resistance uses up willpower and raises my anxiety, making it likely that I'll binge on picking later. I'd rather gather data about what helped or didn't, and then try to meet my underlying needs again when the next urge arises.

It isn't a perfect system. I'm continuing to learn what meets each kind of need, and there may be more needs that I haven't discovered yet. In the meantime, I want to face my failures with curiosity and compassion. An urge to pick is a message from my body, and I'm trying to learn its language.

Through writing publicly about my struggle with dermatillomania, and answering questions from others who share my experience, I realized some additional strategies and mindset shifts that may help.

First, protective barriers (such as bandaids, gloves, or hats) are helpful, in a limited way: They can help you notice what you're doing. They won't prevent it entirely, because it's too easy to remove them or find something else to pick. But if you find yourself picking accidentally or unconsciously, barriers may slow you down enough to choose another action—to meet the needs that created the urge.

Second, punishments and rewards are unhelpful, because they force you to depend on willpower. I'm grateful that my family understood this, and trusted me when I said I couldn't help myself, even though none of us knew about my autism at the time. I was often harder on myself than they were, inventing my own incentives without realizing how that only increased my stress.

Third, success or failure in this area has nothing to do with virtue. Self-control, like joy or peace, is the fruit of other actions, not something you can generate out of thin air. If this habit causes you any shame, remind yourself that it's rooted in needs, as natural as hunger or tiredness, and you're on a path to find healthier ways to meet those needs.

Fourth, you're not alone. You're sharing this journey with many others—including me.

6

Relationships

How I Get Along with People

I once met a woman who asked me for advice to help her autistic son build strong relationships. She said he had an active social life online, but not in the "real world."

I encouraged her to see the Internet as part of the real world, and treat online friendships as real friendships. Yes, interactions there can pose a risk if the match isn't appropriate. The same is true in person. But both places offer amazing opportunities for fulfilling friendships, too.

As a child, I usually had no more than one or two friends at a time. My first real "friend group," on the other hand, was through an online forum. There, fans of the show *Kim Possible* created art, music, and scripts for new episodes, including ourselves as characters. We formed a tight-knit, supportive community around our shared interest, and nicknamed ourselves "Tomers" since the forum was called *TV Tome*.

When the Academy Awards aired, we designed awards for one another, and I was voted "Nicest Tomer." I printed the award and hung it in my high school locker, to remind myself of this group of friends who valued me.

I sincerely believe it would not have been possible for me, at that age, to have an equivalent experience in person. I did later, in college. But first I needed practice with communicating asynchronously, through written messages and creative collaboration—without the complexity of reading facial expressions, catching sarcasm, and processing audio fast enough to laugh at jokes in time.

My lack of skill in those areas, and lack of access to autistic friends who communicated like me, led me to have few friends at school. At one point I had none at all, after one phoned me to say that she wanted to stop being friends. Her reason? All the other kids thought I was uncool.

That was in elementary school, but middle school was the hardest. I remember classmates talking to me out of pity—I could tell it was out of pity—and I remember savoring those crumbs, even though the same sort of attention with the same condescending attitude would have offended me a few years earlier.

I think the most important thing in that situation, more important than actually making friends, is holding on to the hope that things will get better. If I knew for a fact that I'd have no friends for months, but then would meet some lifelong friends, how would I have spent my time alone? Probably more on hobbies, and less on self-deprecation.

And it was through hobbies that I eventually made friends, both online and in person. I found them not by looking for friends, but by focusing on what I loved, such as reading and dance—and discovering who else did, too.

Masking

By the time I graduated from college, I had a solid grasp on how to make and keep friends, but not how to prevent strangers and acquaintances from giving me odd looks. I acquired that skill a few years later, and I'm not sure it was entirely a good thing.

It happened in my early twenties, when I spent a summer living and working in Europe. I took more selfies that summer than in my entire life before. It felt meaningful, as a way to stay connected with friends back home. But to give them an accurate window into my world, I needed a skill I'd never practiced before: Making my face look the way I feel.

Through lots of trial and error, I learned which muscles on my face match which expressions in a photo. Now, a posed photo of me looks almost as good as a candidly captured moment of joy. But, like one bite from a tree of knowledge, I can't undo that awareness. The mere presence of other people gives my mind a preview of what my face is doing. I feel uncomfortable if it's inaccurate, such as a blank look when I'm actually interested, and I've gotten into the habit of manually correcting it.

Awareness of my face led to awareness of other ways I might be perceived, too. I learned how to murmur "hmm" and "yeah" at appropriate moments to indicate interest, and lilt my naturally monotone voice to keep others interested in my words as well. I learned to periodically check for reactions instead of dissociating into the world of the story I'm telling.

But I find all of this utterly exhausting. My friend Joel compares it to holding a chair at arm's length in front of you, while simultaneously trying to carry on a conversation. What stim suppression does to the body, communication control does to the mind—and "masking" is a word that I've heard autistics use for both.

However, I think the metaphor of a mask can be misleading. It sounds like I'm being deceptive, or changing who I am to fit in, whereas I'm actually just trying to wear my true feelings on my face. I see it more like a language—a way to communicate. Yes, it can feel stressful and unnatural to speak a new language. It requires extra concentration, and it's easy to make mistakes, but it can also be useful.

It becomes more of a problem when the effort is one-sided. Communicating across neurotypes is like communicating across cultures— one side shouldn't have to constantly adapt everything about how they communicate just to be understood. So, I look for opportunities to translate my language:

◇ My closest friends know that the more focused I am on explaining a complex idea, the more monotone I'll become, and the less I'll be able to pay attention to their reactions. But they also know that once my thoughts are out, I'll be eager to hear theirs.

◇ My co-workers know that stimming helps me focus, and they don't judge me for using a fidget toy during meetings.

◇ My family knows that even if I'm not looking at them, I'm still listening.

In a perfect world, all communication styles would be understood well enough that no one would need to mask or translate. But in the meantime, before I have the chance to explain my motivations, I always hope people will trust that my intentions are good.

Neurodivergent Friends

I have wonderful friends of many neurotypes now, but I still find it easiest to be myself around people who aren't neurotypical.

Years ago, before I knew I was autistic, I spent eight months living in a highly neurodiverse house. Most of my housemates had ADHD, PTSD, bipolar, autism, or some combination of those. I might have been the only one who didn't realize I was neurodivergent—that is, not neurotypical.

In that house, for the first time since childhood, I didn't feel like an introvert. I got energy from being around people, because I didn't feel the need to play a role—I could just be. Stimming was common and accepted. People dressed however they liked. Meltdowns were an occasional part of life, not a big and scary event.

Moreover, diverse strengths were recognized and celebrated. I embraced any form of categorizing, from putting away clean dishes to organizing the entire garage. Others took care of cooking food, washing dishes, tending the fire, and mowing the lawn—all things that I found hard for cognitive or sensory reasons.

I treasure the memory of that house as a taste of what's possible when a variety of neurotypes come together. The whole house eventually shifted to new tenants, but I was one of the first to go. I moved out to escape the only negative part of an otherwise perfect environment—the pain of unrequited love.

Heartbreak

Through the years, most of my attempts at a romantic relationship have flopped. The emotional fallout was always intense, far more than I feel able to convey from the vantage point of my presently healed heart. But in losing access to the fresh, raw pain of heartbreak, I've gained the ability to analyze it. I've come to recognize at least three autistic traits that affect how I process heartbreak:

◇ **Special interests**, or topics of intense fascination, can cause me to highly value others' happiness, presence, or mere existence, sometimes even more than my own wellbeing. I've read that for autistic women and girls, special interests often include people or characters. This explains my desire to learn as much as possible about those I love, and also why rejection strikes so deeply. I wish I'd known that my awe is caused as much by my own neurology as it is by another person's admirable characteristics.

◇ **Solid expectations** mean that my brain is not naturally prepared for transition, and unexpected changes can hit like a load of bricks. Everything is easier to handle if I have time to mentally prepare, but if I don't see a major change coming, it can feel devastating. Heartbreak in particular has often surprised me, because my struggle to read nonverbal cues has hidden the clues leading up to it. As I've gotten older, I've learned to keep in mind that things can always change, but that wasn't my default narrative—it's one I had to learn from experience.

◇ **Repetitive thoughts**, technically called "perseveration," can amplify both interests and memories. Perseveration causes me to remind myself, again and again, that I've lost someone I loved, and that things didn't go as I hoped. Before I found out that this is a common autistic trait, I didn't fight such thoughts, because I believed they were justified. When I began to recognize how it can deepen and prolong emotional pain, though, I started to handle all kinds of grief differently. I now see the value in setting aside periods of time specifically to process it, and then trying to redirect any painful thoughts that arise outside those times.

I believe that the principles I've learned from numerous heartbreaks can apply to any sort of loss. Even understanding why I feel the way I feel is a comfort in itself.

Flirting

One reason that I've historically struggled with initiating romance is that I often have trouble reading between the lines, especially when it comes to flirting.

I remember, as a teenager, being at a lake with some other teens. The boys kept trying to push the girls off the dock—except me, whom they ignored—and the girls kept squealing and running away.

Unexpected water is torture to me, and there was no way I could let a fellow girl go through that while it was in my power to keep her safe. So I said to the girls, "Stay by me, I'll protect you!"

They didn't, of course. They pretended not to hear my generous offer, suffered the consequences, and then complained loudly about it. I thought they were being ridiculous, but I would have respected their decision if they'd simply stated the truth: "Thanks, but we don't actually want the boys to stop pushing us. The water isn't that bad, and it's worth the risk for the attention we're getting."

The hidden logic of their actions escaped me at the time, but dawned on me years later. I wish I'd made an effort to discover their reasons, and I wish they'd made an effort to discover mine, too.

Mutual Understanding

If others were mysterious to me, I was at least as mysterious to them. Twice, I've been called an enigma. Both times were by guys interested in dating me, a rare occurrence that I didn't know how to handle at the time.

Maybe they found it enigmatic that I did flirty things for non-flirty reasons, like getting excited about common interests or holding eye contact for too long. My complete incompetence at the neurotypical dance of flirting left them with mixed signals. But if they had asked me a straightforward question, then I could have easily answered.

My relationship with Jake was founded on straightforward questions. In the past four years, our questions and answers have grown deeper—more intimate, more intricate—but we've never wavered from the honest pursuit of mutual understanding. I finally feel knowable, and known—no longer a puzzling enigma.

I was diagnosed with autism just one year before meeting Jake. It's easy for him to forget that those events happened so close, since talking about each other's brains is an important part of our relationship, and

I'm always analyzing mine through the lens of autism. The timing is more salient to me, however, since I believe that discovering my autism gave me tools to build a good relationship.

One day, when Jake was reminded of the timing and surprised by it anew, I said, "Yeah, I think a lot of my problems with previous relationships were caused by not knowing—"

I was going to say, "common pitfalls of my communication style," or "how to identify and articulate my unique needs," or "how vastly different other brains can be," or something else that I didn't understand in the preceding ten years of consecutive heartbreaks.

"—not knowing how great you are?" he interrupted. It took me a while to recover from the overwhelming sweetness of that response, but when I did, I recognized the wisdom in it.

For so long, I had clung obsessively to the objects of my affection, mentally if not physically, afraid that I would never be exactly what they wanted. That kind of fear, while difficult to control, is not conducive to the kind of open conversations that form the bedrock of a secure relationship.

Through learning about autism, I came to know myself. Through knowing myself, I came to accept myself. And through accepting myself, I was more prepared to enter a healthy relationship when an amazing person for me came along.

7

Misunderstandings

How People Get Me Wrong

What is it like when autistic people spend time together, with no one else around? Not every autistic group is the same, but here's what I've experienced with the friends who helped me discover my autism.

People might think that we go off on long tangents, leaving our listeners to suffer in boredom. But hiding boredom out of politeness is a neurotypical custom. When I'm with autistic friends, and one is talking, those who are genuinely interested keep listening, and the others spontaneously start side conversations with no hard feelings. It's considered rude to fake interest, and kind to encourage others to pursue what stimulates their minds.

People might think that the timing in autistic conversations is awkward for everyone involved—speakers who get interrupted, and listeners who can't figure out when it's okay to interrupt. But figuring that out from tone alone is what neurotypical minds do. When I'm with autistic friends, we devise systems to identify a good time to speak. I hold up one finger when I think of something to say, two fingers if I'm second in line, and so on. When the next person starts to talk, everyone after them drops a finger, to show that they're moving up the line. This may sound hard to track, but we find it way easier than subtle cues woven into the rhythm of speech.

People might think that autistics misunderstand one another, because of our tendency to use phrases out of context, sometimes not realizing that more information is needed to interpret our words. But processing information at the moment it's delivered is a neurotypical expectation. When I'm with autistic friends, we're constantly asking one another what we meant—was it this meaning, or this other slightly different meaning? Carving up our communication, uncovering its deeper layers of precision, is a satisfying art form, as well as a safety net of mutual understanding.

This is only the experience of one autistic woman with one group of friends. However, multiple studies have shown that autistic people generally do communicate better with one another than with neuro-typical people. This has been called the "Double Empathy Problem." It's not just a matter of personal comfort—people who share the same neurotype are able to interpret one another's words more accurately.

Autistic misunderstandings are caused less by how we communicate, and more by a mismatch between us and other neurotypes. Every time I was misunderstanding someone, they were also misunderstanding me.

Internal Experiences

My first encounter with autism in literature was through a novel written by a neurotypical author for a neurotypical audience. In it, she gets many things right about autism, and many things wrong.

The external behaviors are spot-on, maybe not for all autistics but certainly for many: Stimming, special interests, blank facial expressions, lack of speech in some circumstances, and unintentional breaking of misunderstood rules. Moreover, those actions aren't random—the character is responding to situations in ways consistent with my own experience. I'm also impressed by the authenticity of how various other characters react, ranging from fear to disdain to genuine efforts to connect.

However, all of that is overshadowed by the narrator's assumptions about the autistic character's internal state. They are assumed to be childlike, living in their own simple world, unfazed by taunts and teases. If I were within the world of the book, I would feel like shouting, "They understand so much! They feel so much! Stop acting like they're a mythical creature who gazes at reality through frosted glass!"

Some books get it worse, I know—and some get it better. I want to add to the growing list of stories that show how autism feels from the inside.

Same Action, Different Meaning

In grocery stores, it takes all of my attention to successfully navigate my cart without running into people, while also making decisions and dealing with all the audio and visual information. It's hard to do all that and also make eye contact and smile at people, so my default demeanor could easily be perceived as rude.

I wish everyone understood that my actions reflect what's happening in my senses, not what's happening in my heart. To be fair, if a neurotypical person acted like me in a grocery store, it would likely mean that they were feeling annoyed—but the same action can have a different meaning for different neurotypes.

I especially notice this distinction when I hear someone say, "Let me finish!" If the person is autistic, it usually means an interruption has threatened to derail their train of thought. I sometimes say it out of desperation, begging for permission to rescue the ideas quickly slipping from my mind.

On the other hand, people who are neurotypical often seem to say it out of annoyance, followed by, "Everything will make sense in a minute if you just keep listening"—as if my interjection were a sign of childish impatience. But when I interrupt, it's never out of impatience. Sometimes it's because I failed to notice a better moment to enter the conversation, but more often it's genuine confusion due to missing some information that would put everything else into context. In that case, letting someone finish means memorizing the nonsensical sounds, then replaying them back to myself once I have the key to unlock their meaning.

So, what should we do? Give autistics the right to finish, and withhold that right from everyone else? No, just be mindful that someone's internal state may be different than you expect, and different than you'd feel if you were acting like them.

Misunderstandings at School

As a student, my motivations were often misunderstood by teachers. For example, many of them interpreted my frequent questions as a sign that I wasn't listening.

Sometimes, when children repeat questions, it means that they weren't listening to the answer. Sometimes, when autistic children in particular repeat questions, it means that they're seeking reassurance instead of information. But both of these explanations only apply to questions that have been fully answered. Throughout my childhood, whenever teachers accused me of "repeating questions," it was always because they'd missed the point of my question. I didn't know how to articulate the difference between the question they'd answered and the question I'd wanted them to answer, so every attempt to rephrase made me sound like a broken record.

Years later, I figured out that it helps to begin by telling people which question they did answer. This shows that I understand why they feel like they've finished answering my question, before I then circle back to the part that they missed. I wish I'd learned this strategy as a child, but I also wish teachers had been more patient with me. What seemed like inattention was really just confusion, and what seemed like an impertinent demand was a fumbling attempt at self-advocacy.

A specific question that frequently caused repercussions at school was, "Is there any homework tonight?" Whenever I asked this, it was treated as an attempt to create extra work for my classmates or earn praise from my teacher. In reality, I was only trying to protect myself from the shame and consequences of having missed an instruction.

Ironically, the shame I was trying to avoid often came anyway, in the groans of classmates and the mockery of teachers. My worst teachers punished my efforts at self-protection by teasing, "Oh, you'd like homework? Well, now that you asked..."

But my best teachers solved this problem through consistency. Either the homework followed a predictable pattern, or it was posted in a predictable place so that no questions were needed—and if I did end up needing to clarify something, those same teachers were the ones who didn't mind.

The Importance of Everything

Sometimes misunderstandings arose at school because of questions I never thought to ask. I wish I'd asked my teachers how long I should be spending on homework each night, then measured the actual time to see how it compared. Although many teachers appreciated my thoroughness and creativity, I'm certain that my homework time far exceeded their intentions, leaving me with less time than my classmates had for sleep and hobbies. It wasn't because I had trouble understanding the work, but rather because of everything feeling equally important.

The truth is, when it comes to homework, not everything is equally important. It's often okay to skim text for answers to questions, instead of reading every word. It's also okay to study until you feel confident you can get 90% on a test (or 80% or 70%), not 100%. And "try your best" doesn't mean doing the maximum you can possibly imagine—it just means making a diligent effort.

I didn't know any of this, because no teacher ever said it explicitly. My parents did express confusion at my workload, and suggested that I might be doing more than necessary, but I needed to hear it from the authority figures who did the grading. Instead, I interpreted directions literally and followed them thoroughly, not reading between the lines to figure out what wasn't necessary.

As an adult, I still struggle to figure out what is and isn't required in various situations. I probably work harder than I need to, because I haven't mastered the art of what to prioritize and what to rush through or skip. I'm conscientious to a fault, because I can't figure out when it's safe not to be. In between "Everybody does that" and "Nobody does that," there's a gray area: "Many do that, and most get away with it."

Speed limits are designed to be broken by up to 10 miles per hour—above that, the consequences begin. I want to learn the equivalent of those 10 miles in other areas of life.

Expressing Solidarity

I've noticed a communication pattern among autistics, myself included—we often try to express solidarity through similarity. "I've been through something like that" is the most natural way for me to tell someone that I support and sympathize with them.

Unfortunately, this pattern contributes to the false stereotype that autistic people lack empathy, because it can make people feel like we're minimizing their struggles by turning the focus on ourselves. For me, though, sharing an analogous story is an expression of empathy—a tangible proof to back up my claim that I can understand how someone feels. It's also an invitation for them to compare and contrast, telling me how their experience differs, so that I can understand them better.

But maybe they feel uncomfortable pointing out where my analogy misses the mark, because that's a form of correction.

Power Moves

It wasn't until my thirties that I learned some people correct factual errors as a power move. That explains why teachers rarely appreciated it when I pointed out their mistakes—they saw it as an attempt to usurp their authority. I also got similar reactions from classmates, colleagues, and others whose authority was equal to mine, because they assumed I was flexing on them.

Nothing could be further from the truth. For me, showing someone where they're wrong feels like keeping them safe from the consequences of their mistake. It's a collaborative pursuit of truth, not a power move.

When autistic people ignore the power games that others play, we sometimes unintentionally threaten their power structures. This explains why bullies of all ages tend to pick on autistic people of all ages. It isn't just that they perceive us as weird enough to make an easy target, but also that we don't pay them the deference they expect.

I'm often too socially oblivious to figure out who has power, or what they want from me. In my ignorance, I sometimes make offhanded comments that invert the hierarchy, or at least equalize it. It's as if I'm the one crying out, "The emperor has no clothes!"—and bullies don't like that. I would have made fewer enemies if I'd learned earlier in life that it can threaten someone's status when you shine a light on their flaws—and that goes beyond just correcting errors.

Making suggestions can imply that a person was doing something wrong. Requesting something can imply that a person neglected to provide that thing already. Offering to help can imply that I don't trust a person's ability. Sometimes, those implications are true. More often, though, it never crosses my mind that someone might read into it that way, until I get a snide reaction.

Refusal Is Communication

When I do something that gets misunderstood, my first instinct is to explain why. The same is true when I can't do something—or I can, but only at great cost to my mental or physical well-being. My justification is partly driven by a wish to be accurately understood, and partly by the myth that I only deserve accommodations if others agree that I need them. But it doesn't always work.

Once, I was asked to do something that I could barely handle. I only agreed to it because I believed it would be brief, which turned out to be false. I tried everything to make my need understood. I asked for help, described my distress, and even tried to find more people to help. But I couldn't stand the idea of outright refusal. I was afraid of causing stress for others, and that fear kept me trapped.

Here's what set me free. I realized that in any memory that causes my heart to shudder, there's a common thread: I didn't stand up for myself. Sometimes, I couldn't. But this time, I could. I saw that defending my right to consent—or in this case, to decline—was the only way to prevent my current stress from turning into a memory that would trigger future stress.

So I did, and it turned out far better than I hoped. I finally found myself free to do what I was best at, and I became a more confident self-advocate in the process. Sometimes, refusal is the only message that will be understood.

Making Peace with Misunderstandings

It isn't always worth the effort to avoid a misunderstanding—and regardless of effort, it isn't always possible. When all is said and done, sometimes I just decide to let people be wrong about me.

When I first read *Jane Eyre*, I saw parts of myself in Jane that I had never seen in a book or movie before. To others she seems prim and precise, simple and stoic—but her heart is actually bursting with intense emotion, and her mind with complex analysis. Few characters can see this, and some assume the opposite is true. But her story taught me that being misunderstood doesn't mean I'm worth any less.

I felt like Jane in a parkour class once, when the instructor asked, "Is anyone confused?" Met with silence all around, he turned to me in particular and said, "Are you sure? You're staring at me with such intensity!"

I was instantly reminded of how Jane "always looked as if she were watching everybody, and scheming plots underhand."

Without missing a beat, I stated, "That's just who I am." The class laughed warmly, as if I'd said something clever, or at least unexpected. I guess no one expects identity as a reason for behavior, but it is. Being autistic deepens my focus on listening and processing, at the expense of calculating an acceptable level of eye contact.

By that point, I had already learned that if people misread my face, it doesn't mean something is wrong with me—it just means they don't speak my language yet. Little by little, I'm learning how to translate.

8

Meltdowns

How I Reach a Tipping Point

Before learning about autism, I used to have mysterious meltdowns. Well into adulthood, I would sometimes break down crying without understanding why, then apologize shamefully for the tears that I couldn't justify.

I still have meltdowns occasionally, but less often, because now I understand what triggers them. For me, it's a combination of too much sensory input and too much cognitive processing, especially when both are surprising.

Once, at a birthday party, I spilled tea on my lap right before the cake was brought out and everyone started singing. Another time, at work, someone wanted me to quickly answer a difficult question while other people were yelling across the room.

Both times, I ended up bawling on the bathroom floor. I let out big, heaving sobs, as if I'd just been betrayed. Both times, I knew that's what I needed. I was fully aware of how little each trigger would matter in the long run, but by that point I'd learned that meltdowns are a physical response, not a reaction to reason. So I gave myself permission to cry, and then time to recover.

My meltdowns look like a cross between a tantrum and a broken heart, neither of which is true. But other autistic people have very different responses to sensory and cognitive overload. Some have shutdowns, becoming inexpressive and withdrawn. Others feel an urgent need for proprioceptive input, throwing their bodies against a wall or floor to drown out the pain. Others yell or run away.

I believe that all of these reactions become harder to handle with the pressure of shame. In my case, a muffled, stifled meltdown is not a recipe for cathartic release, especially when combined with bitterness at feeling trapped by others' expectations. No matter how large the reaction or how small the cause, recovery is smoother with the safety of self-acceptance.

Not Overreacting

A meltdown doesn't always mean that I'm upset. Often, it simply means that I'm depleted.

One afternoon, after five minutes of ordinary conversation with Jake, I collapsed into tears on his shoulder. There had been nothing upsetting about the talk, and I quickly told him so. But there had been lots of multitasking and miscommunication in the previous few hours of work. I didn't realize soon enough that the energy I needed for that five-minute conversation was the last ounce of energy I had.

People often find autistic meltdowns confusing, and ask why we're overreacting to such a small thing. Sometimes, it isn't about the thing in question at all. But even if it is, it's rare for me to consider any reaction an overreaction.

Overdoing something (overthinking, oversharing, etc.) means doing it too much, in comparison to some standard. Before we can agree that someone is overreacting, we have to agree on the standard to which we're comparing them. That standard might be how they would react if they were having a better day, or how most people would react.

But the standard I prefer to use is the size of the feeling. A big reaction to a big feeling isn't an overreaction—it's an accurate reaction. It's only overreacting if it's a big reaction to a small feeling, because then it isn't communicating how the person really feels.

I believe, for those of us who experience life intensely, that under-reacting is much more common. We start out reacting proportionately to our feelings as children, then dampen our expressiveness over time when it repeatedly gets labeled as an overreaction. Still, there are days when I lack the strength to dampen anything, and it all comes out.

Before a Meltdown

Sometimes, I can catch a meltdown before it reaches full force. When that happens, I call it a "mini meltdown." I remember one in particular, when I was talking with Jake and my brain suddenly ran out of space to process the many threads of our conversation. My body reacted by letting out a sharp cry, then curling up and covering my head.

That was the extent of the meltdown, because I knew what to do about it. I said, "I need a whiteboard!" and dashed from the room, returning moments later with the magical device in hand. I curled up beside Jake, who wrapped his arms around my shoulders, leaving my hands free to write. I've heard many autistics say they can't handle touch during a meltdown, and need space instead, but I don't. I feel like my body is spinning out of control, and I want to feel securely pro-tected while I recover from the previous shock.

Jake waited patiently as I surveyed the damage in my mind. There had been a swift avalanche, and I needed to recover three separate thoughts from under the wreckage. The first was easy to spot, and I jotted it down. The second required some searching, but I found it too. The third had only been half-formed when the overwhelm hit, so I stared at it a little longer to make sure it was complete.

With my three thoughts recorded, I was able to turn back to Jake and say calmly, "I'm ready to continue talking now." I then apologized for the sudden outburst, but he assured me that no matter what I do or how confusing it seems, he always trusts that it will make sense after I have a chance to explain.

I'm profoundly grateful for that trust, because there are also times when I feel a meltdown approaching and there's nothing I can do to stop it. When I'm startled, overwhelmed, or in pain, my body sometimes does things I don't want it to.

I've heard that you can't control what happens to you, but you can control how you react. That isn't always true for me. Often, I have more control over what happens to me than how I react to it. I can choose to avoid some stressful situations, and I can choose to exit others. These may sound like reactions, but I see them as proactive, preventative actions. I have less control when I'm reactive, and more control when I'm proactive.

During a Meltdown

I often come across stories where a stranger goes out of their way to help an autistic child through a meltdown. The parent posts the heroic and heartwarming tale on social media, and it goes viral. But these stories frustrate me, because they usually miss why the child was having the meltdown in the first place.

I once read about a child who couldn't sit still on a train. His mom tried to bribe him with candy and force him to sit, but his pent-up energy exploded under the weight of that demand. The mom was very grateful when a police officer stepped in to distract her son from his distress by showing off his gear and striking up a conversation.

When an autistic child has a public meltdown, it means they don't have the strength to handle the environment, the actions asked of them, or both. When someone steps in to save the day, I notice that it's usually by engaging the child with their special interest, helping them move to a calmer place, or just staying present to reassure them that it's safe to feel that way.

When I was little, my dad would do all of these things by taking me outside for a walk. He wouldn't bring up the cause of the meltdown until after we had been walking for a while, noticing and discussing any plants or bugs we spotted along the way.

It can take a lot of self-control to be the calm in the storm when someone you love is having a big reaction to a seemingly small trigger. It's wonderful if your emotions can be an anchor for them to flail around, until they're finally able to collapse into your peace—but if not, that's okay. They have the right to express their feelings, but you also have the right to feel safe. If their storm is stronger than your calm, then time apart protects you both.

The same is true from within the storm. My reactions are a form of communication, but I often find myself among people who don't speak the language of meltdowns or know how to handle them. In that situation, I find that it's better to step away. It takes longer to calm myself without help, but it's necessary if the available helpers are strangers or acquaintances who are likely to misunderstand me when I'm upset.

These are good ways to handle a meltdown. But it's even better to recognize why they happen in the first place.

Reviewing a Meltdown

If it seems hard to figure out an autistic meltdown from the outside, it can be hard from the inside, too. Mid-meltdown is no time for sleuthing, but a later review can help identify causes and avoid them in the future. I prefer to call these causes "ingredients," because it's rarely just one thing. There might be a straw that breaks the camel's back, but only if the burden is heavy already.

Here are three ingredients that may contribute to a meltdown, with questions to help you consider if that ingredient applies to a recent meltdown that you're evaluating.

◇ **Burnout:** Ask yourself, "What unusual circumstances may have sapped my strength in the day leading up to the meltdown?" The answer may include difficult tasks, extra socializing, new environments, unfamiliar foods, or poor sleep. Some call the result "having an empty bucket." Some call it "being low on spoons," a metaphor that I'll discuss more in the chapter on Optimizing. I usually call it "feeling fragile." Whatever you call it, less strength means less resilience, making you more susceptible to a meltdown when new stressors arise.

◇ **Sensory overload:** Another ingredient to consider is intense sensory input. Ask yourself, "What did I see, hear, taste, smell, and feel right before the meltdown?" However, this can be a hard question to answer accurately if you've often been told that your sensory pain is not a big deal. If none of your answers to the sensory question feel like they ought to be a problem, try asking this instead: "What memories do I have of people telling me something shouldn't hurt or is barely noticeable?" If people made fun of you for flinching at raindrops, you might have water sensitivity. If they acted incredulous that you could hear a TV on mute, then you might have audio sensitivity. Unpack what surprises others about you, and you may discover hidden sensory needs.

◇ **Cognitive overload:** Ask yourself, "What new information did I encounter right before the meltdown?" Whatever it was, you may not have been able to process it quickly or thoroughly enough to maintain a feeling of control. Some examples include multitasking, changes of plan, holding multiple steps in memory, quick transitions, and surprises. It also takes mental effort to convert information from one form to another, like if your brain needs to turn verbal directions into a visual map. Something as simple as a question can cause cognitive overload if other ingredients are present. And if every ingredient is small, they can still add up.

Over time, as you learn which ingredients contribute to your meltdowns, you can try to reduce them. The recipe for a meltdown-free day is to eliminate ingredients that your body and brain can't handle.

Accepting the Inevitable

Autistic children who have meltdowns don't grow out of them. Some do stop having them, though.

What's the difference? You "grow out of" something when your brain or body changes. Although all brains mature over time, autistics tend to maintain the capacity for meltdowns. This is a good thing, since meltdowns serve as a safety valve when the pressure gets too high.

If meltdowns remain possible, then why do autistic adults seem to have them less often than autistic children do? We've spent more time learning what we find most stressful, and how to protect ourselves from it. This reduces the need for meltdowns. An ideal environment removes that need entirely, though such environments tend to be temporary.

I still have occasional meltdowns. I prefer to avoid what causes them, but when I can't, I'm grateful for the release. A meltdown may look like an explosion, but it protects me from implosion.

9

Quirks

How Else My Brain Is Different

The more time I spend reading and writing about what it means to be autistic, the more I discover seemingly random traits that are shared by many autistic people. Some of these so-called "quirks" are directly caused by well-known autistic tendencies. Others overlap with autism so often that the connection has been researched, even if it isn't listed in the DSM. Others seem unconnected to autism at first glance, if they're even connected at all.

Still, when I describe these experiences, they seem to elicit strong reactions from autistic people who feel the same. So as you read this chapter—and other chapters too, but especially this one—remember that many autistic experiences differ from mine, but also that I'm also far from alone.

Inertia

I often feel some form of inertia—mental, physical, or both. In the scientific sense, inertia means that an object keeps doing what it's doing, either moving or resting, until an external force causes it to change.

In the human sense, inertia also means a natural drive to continue. Here's what that can look like in practice, for me:

◇ It's more interesting to continue learning about one topic, and explore its nuances more deeply, than to branch out.

◇ It's more fulfilling to continue working on a single task, and accomplish it well, than to keep switching between tasks.

◇ It's more comfortable to continue eating the same food, or wearing the same clothes, than to try something new.

◇ It's more effortless to continue doing whatever I'm doing than to switch to anything else.

This experience of inertia would explain the "preference for sameness" listed in the diagnostic criteria for autism. But sometimes, inertia isn't my preference at all. It makes housework very difficult, because that requires me to constantly shift attention from one small task to another. As with inertia in the scientific sense, external intervention helps—the company of another human does wonders to prompt and encourage me.

Mental Modes

I feel like my brain has two settings, which I call "flexible mode" and "safe mode." I can usually choose which one I want to be in, though it takes some time to switch back and forth. Both have pros and cons.

Flexible mode means I'm prepared for surprises and interruptions. I know they can come at any moment, so I stay alert. And when they happen, I can handle them. Safe mode means I'm able to focus, without fear of interruption. I feel protected, because I know that if I begin a complex thought process, it won't get cut off.

The problem with flexible mode is that it doesn't allow me to think very deeply, or do the kind of work I find most meaningful. It also takes a lot of energy, and creates physical tension in my body. The problem with safe mode is that it makes me more vulnerable. If something breaks my concentration, it's extra upsetting, and it makes me lose my ability to think and speak clearly.

I feel calmest and happiest in safe mode, but most of the time it isn't worth the risk. Even though flexible mode is harder, it isn't nearly as hard as suddenly being thrust out of safe mode by an interruption. Everything feels easier if I'm ready for it, but the hard part is remaining ready.

Eye Contact

Many autistics find eye contact painful. I usually don't. It's the multitasking that gets to me. I can only do two of these things at once: Look, listen, plan.

◇ **If I look and listen but don't plan**, then I'll hear what you're saying, but won't have a response ready when you stop talking.

◇ **If I listen and plan but don't look**, then I can carry on a conversation, but may appear distracted.

◇ **If I plan and look but don't listen**, then I feel like I'm being rude. I prefer to pause either my planning or my looking to make sure that I can listen.

Then, when it's my turn to talk, I can pick any two: Look, speak, plan.

◇ **If I look and speak but don't plan**, then I can only get out the words I've already planned. To plan more, I have to look away.

◇ **If I speak and plan but don't look**, I can be quite eloquent, but I may miss your unspoken reactions.

◇ **If I plan and look but don't speak**, it feels like an inefficient pause in the conversation. I prefer to glance away so I can gather my next words more quickly.

I've heard many autistics say, "I can look at you or listen to you, but not both." They say this to prove that it's unhelpful to force eye contact. But for me, it's more complex than that. I can look and listen at the same time when needed, but I spent most of my life not realizing that comes at a cost.

I came across a list of personal goals from ten years ago, and one of them was: "Make better eye contact." I didn't write that because of any negative feedback I'd received. I certainly didn't write it because of any so-called autism therapy—no one knew I was autistic at the time, including me. I wrote it because it's a message that gets sent, from various sources, to everyone: Make eye contact to show that you're listening. Make eye contact to show that you care. Make eye contact to make people like you more.

Never once did that advice come with a disclaimer that there would be tradeoffs. For every moment that I spend maintaining the commonly accepted amount of eye contact—not too much, not too little—I lose a bit of concentration, and I gain a bit of stress.

I'm grateful that no one ever tried to force me to look in their eyes. I'm a little sad that I tried to force myself. But mostly, I'm glad that I understand my brain better now.

Body Language

Not all autistics are completely oblivious to body language. I'm not. I can tell when a raised eyebrow means I've done something odd, a startled glance means I've spoken in an irregular rhythm, or a confused look means I've spouted too many ideas with too little context. But I rarely know what to do about it.

Sometimes, I can apologize. Clarify. Learn. Add new information to my internal database of what people expect. Other times, the reaction is too subtle, and I'm stuck wondering, *Did I actually make a mistake? Will I make things weirder by acknowledging it? If I ask what I did wrong, will they even know how to describe it?*

They probably won't. It seems to me that neurotypical people follow their intuition in most social interactions, basing decisions on years of observation without ever putting those lessons into words. I, on the other hand, need words for everything. Some autistics need pictures. Nearly all of us need practical explanations to illuminate the mysterious magic of intuition. More importantly, we need reassurance that it's okay to make mistakes.

Working Memory

When I'm holding a thought in my mind, and I'm about to act on it soon, the place where it lives is called "working memory." For me, it's a very small place. My working memory can hold one or two thoughts with intense focus and attention, but if I try to juggle three or four at the same time, they all drop.

Thoughts, in this context, could include names in a story, steps to complete a task, pros and cons for making a decision, options to choose from—anything that needs to stay within my awareness to understand what's happening or about to happen.

When my working memory runs out of room, the only way for me to hold onto such thoughts is to write them down and keep them in view. Even in the middle of a conversation, I'm often taking notes. It makes me a better listener—not compared to others, but compared to myself without notes—because I can temporarily set aside my own questions and comments without fear of forgetting them.

I still tend to flinch from complexity. But when I remember to write down my thoughts, it feels like going into battle with sufficient armor to handle the fight.

Perception

Some people perceive sensory input through multiple senses, such as tasting music notes or smelling numbers. That's called synesthesia, and I have a subtle form of it—similar to those who see letters in color, but with extra steps.

Each letter in the alphabet makes me feel a certain way. It's sort of like an aura, but felt instead of seen. Colors also have auras—an emotional experience on top of a sensory experience. And a letter can feel similar to a color—for example, "K" has the same aura as purple.

So, I don't actually see letters in color. But things happen as if I did. I mix up street names if they map to the same color combination, and I don't catch puns if they depend on words that sound alike but are spelled differently.

I also perceive space in an unusual way. When I look around a room, I see lines—or at least, I feel them. What I mean is, the edges of furniture and frames don't stop at the corners. They continue across the room, like straight spiderwebs, intersecting other lines and piercing various objects. This makes it very easy to notice when things are lined up, and when they aren't.

In my own space, you may see me adjusting a chair's position, or pushing a book's spine until it's flush with the others. This clears cobwebs of connection, reducing my visual clutter. In someone else's home, I can easily resist, because such adjustments aren't compulsive, only calming. One exception is to stabilize an object that's precariously balanced, since I can visually measure the distance from its center of gravity to the edge where it may fall.

Spatial awareness, like sensory and social awareness, takes up space in my mind. If I miss sarcasm, or forget to make a facial expression, or run out of energy to make a decision, I'm not saying the lines in the room are to blame—but they do contribute.

How I'm Doing

I've learned that "How are you?" is usually meant as a greeting, not a question. But if I give a trite answer, and the person responds by repeating the question a second time—slower, with emphasis—then I know it's truly a question.

That's when it gets complicated. I used to think I wasn't affected by "alexithymia," or the inability to label emotions. I could write an essay describing my emotions at any given moment, so I must not be alexithymic, right?

Well, I share this similarity: I can't identify my emotions at first glance. I look inside, and it's a complex jumble. If I look closer, though, I can pick it apart. My memories of the recent past, my perception of the current environment, and my expectations for the near future all add up to a collection of distinct, identifiable, and sometimes contradictory emotions.

To honestly describe how I'm doing, I have to list each fact that's hovering in my thoughts, and then say how that fact makes me feel. Essentially, I'm pretending that the question isn't, "How are you?" but rather, "What's taking up space in your brain?" A few friends have even started phrasing the question that way, which helps me to know when they want a thorough answer.

Some autistic people really are alexithymic. Others, like me, merely access their emotions in an unconventional way.

Reading Aloud

It's pretty common for teachers to have one student read aloud while others follow along in the book, but it's way too much multitasking for my brain. I can only listen if I'm not reading, I can only read if I'm not listening, and I can only track where the current reader is on the page if I'm neither reading nor listening to understand—only matching meaningless letters and sounds.

So, how did I handle it when I was in school? How did conscientious Little Me remain alert enough to pick up at the right spot when it was my turn, while comprehending anything?

I got very fast at reading. That allowed me to spend most of my time tracking the sounds, because I could occasionally ignore the audio for a few seconds while I quickly read ahead. When my turn came to read aloud, I would use the brief pause at the end of each sentence to silently pre-read the next sentence. Then, when I spoke the words, I was equipped with enough context to know where the intonation should go.

I didn't realize what I was doing. I just remember feeling confused about why the other kids were reading in a choppy monotone, instead of emphasizing the important words like a storyteller. My method was a coping strategy that took effort, and still does, but it happens to make me an excellent oral reader.

Focusing on Details

I used to love the phrase "can't see the forest for the trees," because it gave me a way to explain why I often miss the big picture... I focus too much on the details! But "can't see" is inaccurate. It would be better to say it takes me longer to see the forest, because first I see the trees.

I need to see enough of them to know if they meet the minimum quantity for a forest. Then I need to see their arrangement to know if it's organic enough for a forest—as opposed to a driveway lined with trees, or a carefully pruned arboretum. Only after gathering data do I feel confident drawing a conclusion. That, for me, is when the forest appears.

Gender Norms

I enjoy feeling feminine. But I hardly ever feel that way around neurotypical women, who tend to express femininity in ways that I find unnatural and unpleasant to imitate. Long nails, hair in place, even vocal volume, graceful movements, perfectly timed interruptions—I can't keep up, and it's exhausting to try.

I feel most feminine when I'm surrounded by guys of any neurotype. There, I can stand and move in ways that make me feel grounded—feet apart, knees bent and bouncing like a fighter, hands gesturing unpredictably, tone freely intensifying or flattening according to my emotions.

I can do all that around women, too. But it makes me feel more masculine, or at least more androgynous. There's nothing wrong with that, but it feels less like me. What's different about being around men is that it highlights the stereotypically feminine traits that I do have, because such traits set me apart. I'm usually the only one who's twirling around corners, flapping with glee, and squealing whenever I hear a clever joke or useful insight.

Autistic men sometimes act that way, too. On average, the autistic people I've met have seemed more androgynous than the neurotypical people I've met. This applies to both men and women, as well as some who reject gender entirely, or identify as nonbinary. I identify as female, and I want to feel feminine—I just don't want it to feel like a performance.

Musicals

Musicals feel like heaven to me, because they portray a world that solves some specifically autistic problems. For example, I'm not great at reading between the lines to figure out a person's true intentions. Musicals solve this through solo songs that reveal exactly what the character is thinking and feeling.

Also, the real world has very few widely accepted ways to express strong emotions. Musicals solve this by making it normal to sing triumphantly, gesture dramatically, and dance freely.

Perhaps the biggest problem that musicals solve is the unscripted guesswork of human interaction. In a musical, everyone miraculously knows how to exist in harmony with everyone else, giving poetic responses in perfect timing, gracefully falling into sync with one another—all while maintaining the illusion that everything is improvised through a secret mutual understanding.

My brain craves this particular kind of beauty—stimulating yet reassuring, consistent yet novel. I'll never master the lyrics and choreography of the neurotypical world, but life feels a bit more like a musical when I'm around other autistics. I wouldn't describe our interactions as effortless harmony, but we tend to value clarity and freedom of expression—making it easier to talk through misunderstandings, and to give one another space and grace.

Always Prepared

I'm terrified of improvisation, so I often spend more time preparing for things than actually doing them. It feels like building a bridge across a chasm—I could attempt to jump, and sometimes I do, but usually it isn't worth the risk.

When I was working as a teacher assistant, I had to substitute for absent teachers. The first time that happened, it was at the last minute, and I stumbled through the class haphazardly. The second time, I had a few hours to prepare, and the teacher ended up thanking me for so "capably and competently and thoughtfully" leading their class. That was a direct result of my preparation, which was a direct result of my fear.

Ideally, I'd like to wield both powers at once: A drive to enter every situation exceptionally well prepared, and a fearless spontaneity that makes it easy to improvise. Realistically, I think reducing the fear might lower the drive, but that's a balance I'd be willing to accept.

I think it's important to recognize when a weakness is also a strength. That doesn't mean I have to stop calling it a weakness—it can be both at once. But seeing the positive flipside lets me evaluate the trade-offs of change, and identify a balance to aim for, while feeling good about who I am in the meantime.

10

Optimizing

How I'm Creating a Better Life

I have frequent opportunities to cultivate bravery, because so many activities are difficult or uncomfortable for me. One example was when a new friend suggested that we rent electric scooters and ride them around the block. I agreed, but she could tell I seemed nervous, and asked why. I said that I never ride bikes, because it hurts when the air hits my face, and a scooter might feel similar.

"We don't have to do this if you don't want to," she said warmly. "It's totally up to you."

We did it, though. We went slow enough that the air wasn't actually much of a problem, but the multitasking was terrifying—keeping my balance, keeping a steady speed, keeping an eye out for cars, and keeping up with the conversation.

"Are you getting any sort of enjoyment out of this?" she asked. I must not have been hiding my discomfort very well.

"I am doing a hard thing!" I answered. I don't think that sounded like a "yes" to her, but it was. I felt empowered, because I knew that I could stop at any moment, and was choosing to continue anyway. As a kid, participating in activities at school or camp, I didn't always have that choice.

I've heard that bravery isn't the absence of fear, but choosing to do something in spite of fear. When I'm forced into situations that are scary for me, it takes away the opportunity to make that choice. But when I'm encouraged to try something new, and given full freedom to say no, then it's a chance to be brave.

Meeting Needs

However, too much focus on bravery can obscure unmet needs. I used to make a big effort to push through anxiety in uncomfortable situations—I saw that as a kind of self-empowerment, and I collected many songs, images, and phrases to remind myself of it. But the more I learn about the rationale behind autistic fears, the more I try to approach them with curiosity: "Why do I feel this way, and what changes could I make to feel better?"

◇ If the root cause is sensory overload, then I consider ways to muffle sensory input.

◇ If the root cause is information overload, then I make a list of all the relevant facts ("knowns"), to help me identify the gaps ("unknowns") and turn them into questions.

◇ If the root cause is social expectations, then I try to explain my differences ahead of time.

◇ If the root cause is unpredictability, then I research and ask questions to mentally prepare.

Mitigating discomfort has become my first step, so that less bravery is required. Nevertheless, some amount of bravery will always be needed. So, is it worth putting myself in challenging situations to build inner strength? Before learning about autism, I would have given an unqualified *yes*.

However, I now recognize that there's a difference between "stretching my comfort zone" and ripping it open. Challenges need to be big enough to develop new skills, but small enough to keep my brain in a state where it's able to grow—not freezing up or melting down. And if I'm not ready for something today, I might be ready another day.

Noticing Needs

One day, while I was cringing at the thought of putting my cold groceries away in my cold freezer, I had an epiphany: *I can wear winter gloves indoors!* The gloves shielded my hands from the icy packages, and I wondered why I'd never thought of that before.

Moreover, I wondered what caused me to think of it this particular time, and how to spot similar solutions more easily in the future. I realized that for me, it takes four steps:

◇ First, I have to believe that comfort is possible—that discomfort is not inevitable. Whether or not this is fully true, it's a useful frame of mind for getting ideas.

◇ Next, I try to notice what feels uncomfortable. This is harder to do if I skip the first step—I end up feeling anxious without recognizing why.

◇ Then, I think about what might help me feel more comfortable, or look online to see what others have tried.

◇ Finally, if possible, I do that thing.

Some things are going to feel uncomfortable no matter what, but other things have the potential to improve, so I figure that it's always worth a try. I keep experimenting, keep reading how other autistics have overcome similar challenges, and keep looking for ways to feel better. I try to minimize sensory discomfort in any way I can, because small discomforts can add up over time—and so can small improvements.

Energy Budgeting

It's easier to notice what bothers me if I observe how various activities affect my energy level. By "energy," I mean more than just not feeling sleepy—I mean the power to take certain actions, like move or speak or work.

Mine goes up and down. I can do most of the things that I want to, but only some of the time. When I can't, it's hard to convince people who've seen me do it before. Moreover, it's hard to convince myself.

I push myself too hard when I assume that my current self is the same as my recent self. It's not. My abilities fluctuate wildly, a trait I've heard other autistics call "spiky functioning" because of how it would look on a graph. I'm trying to grow more attentive to who I am right now, not twisting it to fit my memory of yesterday.

I'm also trying to budget my energy. This means limiting how many draining activities I do in a day, preparing for those activities through other ones that fill me up, and intentionally recharging my energy after it's drained. It's not magic, just math.

There's no official measurement to quantify the kind of energy I'm talking about, but I like to use the metaphorical unit of "spoons"—as in, each day you get a handful of spoons to spend, and the number varies. That idea was invented by Christine Miserandino, who applies it to chronic illness. But I've seen it used by many autistic people too, due to the number of ordinary activities that require more spoons for us than for others.

Personally, my biggest energy drains are sensory overload, socializing, decisions, and ambiguity. On the flipside, my biggest energy givers are compression and special interests. If I combine an energy giver with an energy drain, then it becomes less draining. For example, it's easier to socialize if I'm sitting between close friends, talking about something that interests me. Later, my favorite way to recover is to lie sideways under a heavy blanket, and research something I'm curious about on my phone.

Procrastination

One big clue that something drains my energy is if I procrastinate doing it. When I try to follow anti-procrastination tips from someone whose mind is very different from mine, it's less likely to help, because procrastination is an outer behavior, not an inner experience. On the other hand, I've learned a lot from people whose motivations for procrastination are similar to mine. Here are some of those motivations:

◇ **Aversion:** I put off a task because I expect it to feel unpleasant. It helps to combine it with something I enjoy, like music or tea.

◇ **Inertia:** I put off a task because I'm caught up in another activity, like I mentioned in the chapter on Quirks. It helps to set a timer, but instead of stopping right when the timer goes off, I use that as a cue to choose a logical stopping point in the current activity.

◇ **Catatonia:** I put off a task because I feel physically stuck when I try to begin. One of my autistic friends breaks out of this feeling using a method she calls "non-repetitive stimming," which looks like trying to wiggle around in a random way. It helps her to speak, and it helps me to get up off the couch when I don't feel like doing the dishes.

◇ **Overwhelm:** I put off a task because I don't know where to begin. The classic advice for this is to break the task down into smaller steps, but what if I have no idea what the first step should be? I find it helps to create a list of any specific questions I have, so that I can search for answers instead of just staring into a cloud of unknowns.

◇ **Distraction:** I put off a task because I forget about it. In the short term, I set timers to check in and confirm that I'm still on track— or get back on track. In the long term, I use to-do lists to keep track of what I intend to do.

◇ **Fear of failure:** I put off a task because the result might suck. This especially applies to emails and phone calls, where I might be judged for awkwardness or accidental impoliteness. It helps to consider the worst that could happen—usually not a threat to my survival—and how likely that outcome is.

◇ **Fear of success:** I put off a task because of what will happen after I'm done—usually another task. I may think I'm procrastinating the first task, but I'm actually procrastinating the second. It helps to recognize when this is happening, because then I can consider what makes the second task scary to me, and find ways to mitigate that.

◇ **Triage:** I put off a task because there's always something more urgent clawing at my attention. It helps to group such tasks into categories (e.g. "tiny non-urgent things" or "home improvements"), then schedule a chunk of time to focus on a particular category. This frees me from wondering if there's something else I ought to be doing instead.

I haven't fully conquered procrastination—but when I do get anything done, it's thanks to these strategies.

Asking for Help

I find it easier to ask for help if I can identify the specific reason I'm struggling. So, a huge benefit of learning about autism was learning the neurological reasons for how I felt, and the vocabulary to explain it. Autism was the missing piece of the script that I now use whenever I need help, which you're welcome to borrow:

- ◇ "Autistic people often…" (Mention a general trait.)
- ◇ "Since I'm autistic, I…" (Give a specific example of the general trait.)
- ◇ "This makes it hard for me to…" (Say what's difficult for me.)
- ◇ "I would find it easier with…" (Describe an accommodation that helps me.)
- ◇ "Is that possible?" (You can use stronger wording here if you prefer, but I like to start with this.)

That's what I say to people who already know I'm autistic. If they don't, and I don't feel comfortable telling them, I go right to what I find difficult, without giving a reason, like: "It's hard for me to figure out how to prioritize my various job responsibilities. I would find it easier with a list, written in order. Is that possible?" However, when people don't know I'm autistic, they often have more trouble understanding the importance of my request.

Learning Patterns

Sometimes, the biggest help someone can give is to gently point out patterns that I might otherwise miss, such as:

- ◇ **If** I talk at length about my interests, **then** some people might believe I don't care about theirs.
- ◇ **If** I correct minor factual errors in a conversation, **then** the person I'm correcting might feel belittled.
- ◇ **If** I try to push through discomfort in a public place, instead of

escaping to a quiet corner to rest, **then** I might unintentionally burst into behavior that confuses bystanders.

None of these are rules. They're only patterns that are useful to notice. Autistics have a reputation for being good at pattern recognition, but that doesn't apply to all patterns. There are some that I need help spotting, like motivations that commonly drive other people's behavior.

I appreciate it when friends or family who are neurotypical—or at least, a different kind of neurodivergent than me—say, "Here's what may be happening from the other person's perspective." That's useful data. Factoring in how others feel, along with how I feel, helps me form a more complete picture of a situation.

I prefer data over advice, because it gives me more autonomy to optimize my own life. I can then decide whether I care enough about a possible "then" to make any changes to an "if." Sometimes I do. Other times I don't, because sometimes it's worth the risk.

11

Uplifting

How to Support People Like Me

The saying goes that you should always be kind, because you never know what someone is going through. Well, you never know perfectly... but there can be clues. If someone is speaking or moving in a way that seems odd or unpredictable to you, there's a chance they may be on the autism spectrum. Like many autistics, I often go through sensory discomfort, information overload, and the fear of being misunderstood. Therefore, being kind to me means being calm, precise, and patient.

You've met someone who's autistic and knows it. You've met someone who's autistic and doesn't know it. You've met someone who tries to hide their autism. You've met someone who wants to explain their autism, but lacks the time, the words, or the bravery.

Autistics only seem rare because some get sent to separate schools, some hide it due to fear of discrimination, and some never realize they're autistic at all. But autistic people are all around you—secretly or openly, self-aware or unaware. If you want to be kind to us, then the only way is to be kind to everyone, giving the benefit of the doubt when people behave in ways you don't understand.

What does that look like in practice? It means approaching others with respect and curiosity, trusting that their actions have reasons, no matter how mysterious they seem at first glance—similar to how you might act in a new country, with different customs and ways of communicating.

Curiosity

Parents of autistic children often tell me that my self-reflective posts help them understand their kids better. On the one hand, this encourages me a lot. I've always been curious about my own mind, so it's been incredible to connect with others who also take an interest in it.

On the other hand, it breaks my heart that so much of the information I share seems to be new to people. It was new to me too, a few years ago, but it wouldn't have been so surprising if I'd spent more time learning from the few autistic people I knew. I could have asked:

◇ "What things seem easy to others, but feel hard to you?"

◇ "What things feel really good to you, even if they seem to serve no other purpose?"

◇ "What things would be helpful to you, if people knew you needed them?"

If you have autistic kids, or autistic friends, and you've never asked them such questions, then I encourage you to do so. It may take a while for them to think of an answer—from minutes to days to years of self-discovery. It may be easier for them to answer in writing, or through a communication device, both of which require practice. But feeling understood can be life-changing, so it's worth the effort.

Support

Although I believe it's always best to learn from the autistic people you know personally, there are some default principles you can start with—support needs that many autistics share. Here are the requests I make whenever friends ask how to support me:

◇ **Allow me to stim.** I feel so much calmer when I know that it's okay for me to fidget, rock, or move in other repetitive ways.

◇ **Be patient.** I may need a little extra time to form my thoughts into words, or to transition from one activity to another.

◇ **Create calm spaces.** If a place is loud or crowded, then I want to escape. In a place that's calm and familiar, I can relax.

◇ **Discuss directly.** I'm not great at reading between the lines. If you appreciate something about me, or need something, or have a suggestion, just say so.

◇ **Encourage my interests.** If I'm excited about a hobby or topic, then it's always on my mind, so I love being able to talk about it at any opportunity.

◇ **Forgive awkwardness.** I might act or speak in unusual ways, but please understand that I'm not trying to make you uncomfortable.

◇ **Give notice.** Unpredictability is stressful. If you let me know your plans ahead of time, I can prepare for them.

Those are some general support ideas that apply across multiple contexts. Additionally, here are some ideas for specific contexts.

At Work

In the workplace, I find that I get along better with colleagues and supervisors if they understand a bit about how my brain works. These are the main items I find it helpful to explain, saving the label of "autism" for the end so that I have a chance to build up to it before any stigma enters their minds.

◇ I have a disability, which is also in some ways a superpower. It affects how I process information, which in turn affects everything else.

◇ I notice tiny details. If anyone needs help double-checking something, I'm a great person to ask.

◇ Since I'm so focused on details, I sometimes miss the big picture. I need help to prioritize and identify what's worth my attention.

◇ I do my best work when I avoid interruptions. If I lose my train of thought, it takes some time to get back on track. But I'm capable of very complex tasks when I focus on them.

◇ I take instructions very literally, not reading between the lines or guessing at what's implied.

◇ Bright lights and loud sounds feel extra bright and loud to me, so I try to block them out when possible.

◇ I have trouble processing audio, so meetings and phone calls can feel draining for me. I need time before to prepare, and time after to recover.

◇ Since I try to follow rules closely, I get confused if they're ignored in practice. I like knowing exactly what's expected of me.

◇ Sometimes I fidget with a small object. It calms me, and helps me to think more clearly.

◇ These things are true because I'm autistic. Many of them are true for other people too, but all are more common for autistics.

At School

Everything on the workplace list is equally valuable for teachers to know, because teachers are working with students toward the goal of learning. But teachers can also benefit from learning about the misunderstandings that arise when an autistic child sees everyone as an equal—including the teacher. My chapter on Misunderstandings contains many examples of this, but a consistent theme is that what feels like a threat to your authority may be driven by a pure intention.

Teachers can also help facilitate inclusion. Passive inclusion is when I walk in a room and nobody kicks me out—but active inclusion is when I walk in a room and people make space for me, physically open their circle to include me, welcome me by name, and catch me up on the current topic of conversation so that I have enough context to participate. The difference is night and day. For classmates who haven't yet befriended autistic students and gotten to know them, active inclusion is a good first step.

Sometimes, time away from school can be more beneficial than any possible improvements at school. Twenty years ago, in the dead of winter, I was a miserable middle schooler—anxious, friendless, and too smart for my own good. My parents pulled me out of school for a week, and took me somewhere new. I'm pretty sure that week single-handedly saved my mental health.

We drove and drove, crossing state borders until the air warmed up enough for shorts and t-shirts. We pitched a large tent by the ocean, and a mini one next to it for storage.

I still had schoolwork to do. But here, it was different. Early each morning, I crawled into the mini tent, sunlight filtering through, and did my assignments one by one. I felt calm, focused, and free, empowered by how much faster I could do them alone than in a classroom. Then I swam, and became friends with the girl from the campsite beside ours, and played checkers by the light of camping lanterns until the stars came out—more stars than I'd ever seen before.

After we returned home, everything slowly got better. I think it's important to notice when rejuvenation is more necessary than participation. This could come in the form of a vacation like mine, a "staycation," or even a switch to homeschooling.

In the Community

Would it be useful to announce my autism on a medical bracelet? What would that say about me? Well, I know what I wish it would say.

I wish it would say to police officers, "I strictly follow every rule to the best of my ability. If it seems like I'm not following directions, it's because I process audio more slowly under stress. Either that, or I feel confused because what you're saying contradicts what I thought I was expected to do. Please slow down, assume the best, and rephrase your words if I seem to have misunderstood."

I wish an autism bracelet would say to paramedics, "I don't know what's happening, and I find that terrifying. Please tell me where we're going, and exactly what to expect. Also, many kinds of physical sensations are uncomfortable for me, and that can be hard to distinguish from pain, so I may not know how to answer when you ask me if something hurts."

To doctors, dentists, mechanics, and other professionals, I wish an autism bracelet would say, "Please explain everything in detail, without skipping information that you assume is common knowledge. List every step I need to take, and include reasons for any recommendations you give. Regardless of how clearly and directly you think you've communicated, please understand that I may still need to ask follow-up questions."

I wish that's what "autism" meant at a glance. But it doesn't. For a lot of the public, autism means that a person will behave unpredictably, won't understand anything, and might do something dangerous. I hope that this perception changes over time. "Autism awareness" campaigns usually focus on spreading reminders that autism exists, but I wish there was more focus on how autistic people think, act, and feel. Then, I could wear it on a bracelet with confidence.

At Home

My parents did a lot of things right.

They told me "I love you" from morning till night, with every hello and every goodbye. Their actions proved it too, but I wasn't the sort of child who could infer hidden messages, so I appreciated the clear words. I always returned them, too—a warm and happy ritual.

My parents celebrated all of my gifts, including ones that other people sometimes laughed at. I still have a tiny sweatshirt that they ordered for me, custom-stitched with the words "Little Miss Precise" in pink cursive.

My mom gave me lots of tips to connect better with friends and succeed at school. My dad acted as if I was perfect and didn't need to change a thing. I think I needed that balance to grow into a competent and confident adult.

My dad turned a giant cardboard box into a miniature office for me, with a fold-down desk and a carpeted floor. It became a cozy, safe space for me to escape to, especially since I could see people coming from a periscope he put in the roof.

My mom read me bedtime stories each evening, after discussing my day. Then, right before saying good night, she always sat with me an extra two minutes. I knew she wouldn't leave until the full two minutes were up, even if we stopped talking and just snuggled, and that predictability felt so peaceful.

There are many ways my life could have been better if I'd learned about autism earlier—but I don't want to give the impression that everything was hard, or that my parents weren't doing the best they could with the information they had. The main piece of information they were missing was that I was sometimes unable to do what they asked.

I was trying my hardest to be good. Sometimes I broke rules I didn't understand. Other times I felt overwhelmed and unable to control my actions. My parents thought I was being defiant on those occasions, but that was never my intention. The pain of misunderstanding made getting in trouble even worse.

We've talked about it now, through hugs and tears. They remember how obedient I was most of the time, and how helpless they felt when occasionally I wasn't. If I couldn't behave, and I couldn't explain why, they didn't know what to do. Now, they wish they had helped me get away to a quiet place, given me time to gather my thoughts, listened to how I felt, and calmly discussed the problem.

If you're a parent, your children may also grow up to realize things that they needed and didn't know how to request. Any time you wonder if you did something wrong, remember that you were (and are) still learning their love language—and also doing a lot of things right.

Regulating Emotions

What looks like defiance is often just dysregulation in disguise. It indicates that someone is having trouble with self-regulation, and the best way to support them in that moment is through co-regulation.

What does all of that mean? Regulation essentially means control—but while "self-control" is about the ability to control outer actions, "self-regulation" is more about the ability to control inner feelings. In practice, this can look like calming yourself down after a stressful event, working up the courage to face a new challenge, or spinning joyfully without falling over. There are no bad emotions, but being regulated means you're able to control your emotions to suit the things you need to do.

Dysregulation, on the other hand, is what happens when the tables turn and your emotions control you. It's not that you're "letting" them, it's that they're just too powerful to handle—running wild, unregulated. They take over your heart rate, movements, breath, and voice.

Co-regulation is when someone helps you feel the way you want to feel, by feeling that way themselves, nearby. They pull you into their calm if calm is what you need, or pump you up to get going if going is what you need.

It's a whole lot easier to regulate emotions with the help of co-regulation than with self-regulation alone. It's also how you learn to self-regulate in the first place. The voice of reason in your head, giving you ideas for how to feel better, is an echo of anyone who helped you do that in the past.

It takes time to understand what dysregulation looks like, in yourself or in others, and even longer to learn what helps, since it varies by person. But it's so valuable, because it lays the foundation for other forms of support.

Neurodiversity

Many of the problems faced by autistics spring less from our autism and more from how others react to it. We live in a world where other people make the rules for what counts as "normal" behavior, so it can create tension if we break those rules by accident, don't understand them to begin with, or aren't able to follow them even when we want to.

Autistic brains follow different rules, and thrive better in environments where we have freedom—to move around, avoid eye contact, write instead of speak, ask lots of precise questions, and stay away from spaces that are too loud or bright. Treating our experiences as valid—not as "too sensitive" or "too literal"—frees us to focus more attention on what makes us come alive.

Treating others as you'd like to be treated works if they want exactly what you want, but no two people think exactly alike. When possible, I prefer to treat others as *they* would like to be treated. A person's neurotype can sometimes imply what they're likely to prefer, but kindness requires curiosity about their individual preferences.

This variety of preferences, perspectives, and processing styles is called neurodiversity. It's a fact, but it's also a movement. It means recognizing and celebrating the beauty of all minds, and supporting one another in the unique challenges that we face.

12

Beauty

How My Heart Is Healing

I believe that autistic brains are beautiful—not only from the outside looking in, but also from the inside looking out.

I enjoy the way I hear music, as something infinitely complex and interesting, with favorite old songs sounding new every time. I enjoy the way my thoughts analyze patterns and identify structures that bring order out of chaos. I enjoy the way I notice every lovely little thing in my environment. I enjoy the way textures feel on my skin, simultaneously calming and invigorating—especially tree bark under bare feet when I'm clambering up to a secret space that only I can reach, surrounded by a shelter all dappled in green and gold.

Like me, many autistics see a world full of intense complexity, brimming with wonder. It can be overwhelming sometimes, to take in the breathtaking and the bothersome, the glorious and the grating, the deeply exhilarating and the downright exhausting, all at once.

But over time, we learn to navigate this maze of information and emotions with stimming to calm us, special interests to delight us, and self-advocacy to empower us. And through it all, we try to remember—beyond our appearance, beyond our abilities, beyond our communication or miscommunication—we are beautiful, all the way to our brains.

Not everyone sees the beauty of autism, though. I once met a woman who tried to assure me that autism doesn't define me.

"It does, though," I said.

"It may be ninety-five percent of who you are," she insisted, "but you're still beautiful and amazing."

Still? As if autism were a stain whose influence I had narrowly escaped? Parents like her want to reassure their kids that they are "more" than their autism, not recognizing how beautiful it can be to see the world the way they do, or how much it can affect their identity.

"I need you to trust me about something," I said, forgetting to thank her for the veiled compliment. "Will you believe me?" She nodded yes. "A hundred percent of me is autistic. I'd be a completely different person without it. It makes me who I am—and I love it!" She cheered and gave me a high five.

I fully believe that without autism, I wouldn't be me. One time, a friend asked everyone around the dinner table, "How would you describe yourself in five words?" I couldn't narrow it down to five, so I chose seven: *Driven, linear, delighted, analytical, precise, brave,* and *wholehearted.* That was still in the early days of discovering all that autism means to me, and I didn't yet realize that I could have answered with a single word: *Autistic.*

That realization was sparked a few weeks later, by a question from another friend: "How would you be different without autism?"

◇ I wouldn't be as driven to improve everything, because fewer things would make me uncomfortable.

◇ I wouldn't be as linear in my thinking, because my brain would transition more smoothly between unrelated ideas.

◇ I wouldn't be as delighted by so many things, because my senses wouldn't be as strong, nor my emotions as finely tuned to the effects of my senses.

◇ I wouldn't be as analytical, because my brain wouldn't be structured to make the same kinds of connections that I do now.

◇ I wouldn't be as precise in my communication, because I would more easily be able to read between the lines and infer meaning from vague statements.

◇ I wouldn't be as brave, because fewer things would require courage—like crowds, and small talk, and water on my skin, and ambiguity.

◇ I wouldn't be as wholehearted, because I wouldn't have the devoted focus that's typical of autistic hobbies, interests, and relationships.

Being autistic comes with many challenges, but I wouldn't give it up for the world. This is even true of my sensory sensitivity.

Inseparable Good and Bad

I've met autistic people who wish they weren't so physically sensitive. Personally, though, I believe that my greatest joys are inseparable from my greatest frustrations. Maybe it's possible for music to be euphoric without sirens being torture, and hugs to be heavenly without cold wind being hell—but that isn't a risk I would take.

So what traits, if any, would I eliminate instead? Assuming I can change nothing (or everything) about society and its response to people like me, what would I alter about my own experience of autism? Just one thing: I would like to stop experiencing discomfort as a threat.

I flinch and feel terror at things I know will hurt, and also at their memory. Discomfort and pain are easier for me to handle than the constant vigilance needed to prevent them—and the lingering sense of danger when they're gone. This fear isn't an autistic trait, since I would still be autistic without it. But it's the first thing that comes to mind if you ask me what I would change about my experience of autism, and I can't think of anything else.

Beautiful to Behold

Whenever I've written about autistic beauty, the most skeptical readers have been autistic people themselves—ones who have trouble seeing anything in their brains to celebrate.

I think that calling brains beautiful is similar to calling bodies beautiful, in that it's necessarily subjective. Would every person on earth call your body beautiful? Probably not—it's in the eye of the beholder. But is there someone, somewhere, whose preferences align perfectly with your appearance? Or who might feel that way, if not for cultural conditioning and manipulative media?

Yes, and probably way more of them than you think. When I say that your brain is beautiful, I mean the same thing: There are people who would marvel at your mind, if only they took the time to see it clearly—free from the myths and stereotypes about autism.

Cringey to Behold

Accepting the beauty of my brain is hardest when I see myself on video. It puts a spotlight on ways of speaking and moving that I don't notice from the inside, but that make me cringe when I observe them from the outside. Yet, when I try to identify what turns me off about those mannerisms, the only way I can express it is through exaggerated, mocking imitation.

Where did I pick that up? It must have been elementary school, based on how nonsensical it is to put down something so harmless. I don't remember being teased in that way myself—but I do remember kids making fun of one another, and figures in pop culture, for reasons that were unarticulated but widely understood.

Widely, but not universally. Sometimes people have surprising reactions to things that I labeled as cringey. One example is the song "All Night" by Parov Stelar. Its electroswing melody is playful and high-pitched, like the song "Barbie Girl" by Aqua, which my elementary school classmates used to mock.

In my early twenties, listening to "All Night" felt like a guilty pleasure. I would roll up my windows whenever it came on, instead of blasting it from my car like every other electroswing song. That changed when I saw Parov Stelar live in concert. With the first notes of "All Night," the crowd went wild—and I suddenly realized that the "Barbie Girl" mockers weren't universal arbiters of taste.

Beauty is only in the eye of the beholder—and so is cringe.

Likable to Behold

There are many people who like me, and many people who don't. For most of my life, I figured that one group was wrong, but I could never be certain which one. Either I was likable, and some people just didn't know me well enough to see it, or I was unlikable, and some people were just patient with me.

It took until my mid-twenties to learn that likability is a question of compatibility, not a question of identity. It took another few years to learn that what makes me less compatible with some people, and more compatible with others, is a beautiful neurotype that I would never want to lose.

I now believe that there is no such thing as "being likable" or "being unlikable." If beauty is in the eye of the beholder, then likability is in the mind of the liker.

Annoying to Behold

Most of the times when I could tell people didn't like me, the reason—sometimes given, sometimes only suspected—was that I'm annoying. But I'm not actually annoying, and neither are you.

If the people who felt annoyed by you went away, and you clambered up a hill to watch the sunset alone, sprawling on a soft picnic blanket, warmed by the golden glow—you would not wear an invisible badge tainting your identity with the knowledge that you are actually annoying. Or you might, but it would be a lie.

In my experience, it doesn't help to notice that some people still like you in spite of your "annoying" traits. It helps more to notice that some people like you because of those traits in particular. But what helps me most is to separate the reaction from the traits, and identify what's happening more precisely. For example, I might think:

◇ *I ask a lot of questions, because I value clarity. This person feels annoyed by that, because they value efficiency more than I do.*

◇ *I like to talk about niche interests, because I value them. This person feels annoyed by that, because they value common interests more than I do.*

◇ *I sometimes speak in a monotone way, because I value focusing on ideas, and find it hard to focus on tone at the same time. This person feels annoyed by that, because they value presentation more than I do.*

If you decide that you want to change your actions to get a different reaction, I support you. But do it with the understanding that you're trying to improve the relationship, not trying to fix yourself. Be aware of the toll it may take on your mental health. And if you don't succeed, know that the problem is a difference in values, not a problem with you as a person.

Validation

Beauty, cringe, likability, and annoyance are not intrinsic features. They are all reactions from other people. Those same people might have also questioned the validity of your words and experiences, but here is what I believe:

◇ Your pain is valid. What they said shouldn't hurt—did.

◇ Your intentions are valid. What they said was malicious—wasn't.

◇ Your passions are valid. What they said isn't worthwhile—is.

◇ Your boundaries are valid. What they said is selfish—isn't.

◇ Your life is valid. What they said is tragic—does not have to be.

With exceptions, perhaps. But only you know, and only you can say. Nothing about you is true just because they said so.

Seeing Beauty

Some people can't see my beauty through my awkwardness, but Jake is a consistent exception to that pattern. One time, he said, "You are so cute!" as I was telling him about something exciting, and expressing my excitement in a particularly autistic way—tilting my head, bending my wrists, hiding behind my hands, and generally letting myself move in ways I resist around others.

It amazed me, as it always does, that he accepts and celebrates me just as I am. I told him so, and his response struck me as profound. He said that people tend to feel awkward when they don't know what's expected of them. If a non-autistic person like him sees an autistic person like me break the script of what they're used to, they may not know how to react.

But we know each other. So when I'm being myself, he knows how to react—by being himself, too! If he's confused about something, he asks me about it. If I expected a different reaction, I ask him about it. Neither of us needs to guess.

Jake finds it easy to give me what I need—patience, precision, comfort, and consistency. In the past, when others found that hard to do, it translated into feeling hard to love—not unloved, just hard to love. But everything changes when you meet people who find it easy to give what you need. They don't even have to like you a lot—they just have to see your presence as a feather, the opposite of a burden. It'll make you feel like you're floating, and it'll make you want to show others that they can also be easy to love.

Clarity

My friend Michelle once complimented my ability to build healthy relationships by clearly communicating my boundaries, expectations, and wishes—and asking others for theirs in return. I thanked her, but also laughed, saying that I only have this ability because I'm compensating for my disability. The reason I try so hard to establish clarity is because I'm terrified of ambiguity.

Communication can often feel like an uphill battle, with misunderstandings causing wounds in both directions. But so many years of fighting have made me a warrior for clarity, and it feels nice to finally begin reaping the rewards. It also has caused me to greatly appreciate a particular communication style that seems to come more naturally to autistics:

◇ Telling the truth—precisely, thoroughly, and unreservedly.

◇ Judging by merits and integrity, without regard for status or authority.

◇ Diving past surface-level pleasantries to explore the depths of one another's fascination.

◇ Giving instructions that include every step, without making assumptions about what the listener already knows.

◇ Picking up on patterns that connect the current topic of conversation to other relevant topics.

These are social skills—some of my favorite ones to cultivate in myself and enjoy in others. Autistic people have a reputation for poor social skills, but I see that as merely a difference in preferences.

Acceptance

How can you tell when an autistic person's heart is healing, and shifting toward self-acceptance? As I trade the heavy armor of hyper-vigilant self-preservation for the spinny sundress of safe authenticity, each step forward may seem like a step back.

◇ I may look "more autistic," as I embrace the calming power of natural movements.

◇ I may request more support, as I recognize the cost of facing challenges alone.

◇ I may react more suddenly to defend my eyes and ears from sights and sounds.

When this first started to happen, I was accused of faking it, as if I were molding myself to match my new label. But I was always this way on the inside—now, it's merely coming out.

However, acceptance goes both ways. When I decided to use "Neurobeautiful" as my blog title and pen name, I never meant for it to only describe autism. Instead, it reflects my belief in the beauty of neurodiversity, which includes all brains—neurotypical and neurodivergent.

I wasn't always a fan of neurodiversity, though. As a teenager, I often believed that my unusual way of thinking was the best way, and that other people were just wrong. A turning point came in college, when I read *Cold Tangerines* by Shauna Niequist, who wrote: "I have been surprised to find that I am given more life, more hope, more moments of buoyancy and redemption, the more I give up... The more I let people be who they are, instead of trying to cram them into what I need from them, the more surprised I am by their beauty and depth."

That quote struck me like a chord. I copied it onto a bright yellow piece of paper and taped it to my mirror. I wanted to learn to see that way, feel that way, live that way. Little did I know how much I needed that kind of grace from others, too.

Eventually, I learned that autism is what makes me so different. When I first began writing about how it feels on the inside, I hoped that deeper understanding would lead to wider acceptance. But for me, accepting others didn't actually begin with understanding them. Instead, acceptance came first, creating a safe space to reveal their beautiful, free, authentic selves.

That's what happens when others accept me, too. It enables me to embody the full spectrum of ways that autism colors my brain.

Thanks

Grateful Acknowledgments

Thank you, reader, for becoming part of my unfolding story. You are making the world a better place for me and others like me, simply by learning what it's like to be us.

Mom, Eileen, Sy, Kelly, Salil, and both Michelles—thank you for cradling my newborn manuscript, and nurturing it into a better book through your curiosity and ideas.

Dad, thank you for helping me to make this book more beautiful.

Jake, thank you for so many memories worth writing about.

Stephanie, thank you for capturing my joy in photos.

Erin, thank you for polishing my words.

To anyone who reviews this book, recommends it to a friend, gives it as a gift, or donates it to a library—thank you for helping to spread my story.

To everyone who has supported me financially—through my shop, Patreon, random acts of generosity, or buying this book—thank you for giving me more time to write.

And to everyone who has been reading the posts that evolved into this book—thank you for following my journey of self-discovery. Your comments inspired many of my ideas, helped me refine them, and showed me that they matter. This book would not have existed without your encouragement, and for that I am forever grateful.

Learn More

Sources & Resources

To learn more about various topics mentioned in this book, visit neurobeautiful.com/learn. There, you'll find links to books, articles, research studies, comics, and videos about:

⋄ Adult Diagnosis

⋄ Autism in Jane Eyre

⋄ Autism in Women & Girls

⋄ Autistic Inertia

⋄ Co-regulation

⋄ Double Empathy Problem

⋄ Intense World Theory

⋄ Monotropism

⋄ Predictive Coding Theory

⋄ Spoon Theory

⋄ Synesthesia

P.S.

More Possibilities

If you relate to many parts of my story, then you might be autistic like me. At least, I believe it's worth exploring the possibility, to see if the pattern of self-recognition continues as you learn more.

However, some of my experiences can also happen for other reasons—such as anxiety, introversion, auditory processing disorder (APD), sensory processing disorder (SPD), or attention-deficit/hyperactivity disorder (ADHD). Several of these may be present in the same family, or even in the same person.

Personally, I've found that autism is the best explanation for my experiences. However, I want to end with a reminder that neurodiversity is vast, neurotypes can intersect, and autism is one of many ways to make sense of a life on the human spectrum.

More Books:

neurobeautiful.com/books

Made in United States
Troutdale, OR
06/25/2024

20818435R00072